PRAISE FOR *HEARTBROKEN*

In *Heartbroken*, Roe touches on every kind of marriage, including those where the relationship wasn't good. He nicely describes the various emotions surviving spouses feel from shock, to tears that refuse to stop, to anger, to numbness. Most of us who have lost a spouse felt many of those emotions. Or the pain may have been so deep we temporarily felt nothing.

— Cecil Murphey, widower
and *New York Times* Bestselling author of more
than 130 books including *90 Minutes in Heaven*
and *Gifted Hands: The Ben Carson Story.*

Heartbroken is excellent. Sensitive, comforting, and practical, it will help widows and widowers walk through the valley of grief and begin to heal. I highly recommend it.

—Paul Casale, Licensed Marriage-Family
Therapist and Mental Health Counselor

Gary Roe's *Heartbroken* is a look at the reality of grief that is long overdue. Not only is it a healing tool for those experiencing the loss of a spouse, but it should be required reading for every pastor. I highly recommend *Heartbroken* to anyone experiencing grief or involved with those who are.

—Dr. Tony Taylor,
Senior Pastor, Hilltop Lakes Chapel

Heartbroken will be recommended reading to be used with my clients. As a Licensed Professional Therapist, loss is frequently the presenting problem and often times it has been unresolved from years past. Gary's stories and insight are relatable and relevant to the grieving soul.

—Carrie Andree,
Licensed Professional Counselor

Anyone grieving the death of a spouse will find this book a welcome addition to the challenge of facing life without someone so special. More than a book of platitudes or theories, *Heartbroken* is filled with practical ways to handle this painful and difficult situation. In a simple yet powerful format, Roe brings meaning and inspiration, and facilitates the presence of hope and comfort, all crucial for those who grieve.

— Dr. Craig Borchardt,
President and CEO, Hospice Brazos Valley

Through real life experiences and sound advice, Roe helps grieving spouses navigate the turbulent waters of loss. His caring heart for people shines through his words and allows him to speak honestly in helpful ways. *Heartbroken* will be an invaluable resource to anyone who is grieving or knows someone who is.

— Troy Allen, Senior Pastor,
First Baptist Church, College Station

Heartbroken not only helps in navigating through the emotions of loss but it allows grievers to feel as if we are not alone. Roe has been a hospice chaplain for years and not only understands the process but has the empathy and compassion to feel with his grievers. This book is a must read for anyone who has lost a loved one.

— Kimberly Dafferner,
author, Licensed Master Social Worker

Heartbroken is exactly what one is after you have lost a spouse. There is no other way to sum up how you feel. I just wish I had this book when I lost my husband to cancer. The quotes in this book from others who have gone through this grief process would have been such a help to me. Every person should have this book to guide them as they begin their journey of grief.

— Norma Millsap, bereaved spouse

Heartbroken is a very concise, well-organized, and easy-to-read book that describes, affirms, and validates the uniqueness of the grief experienced by one who has lost a spouse. The insights and interviews given by the grieving spouses offer far more impact than if the author had just described the feelings.

— Eleanor Ford, bereaved spouse

Heartbroken was just what I needed 15 months after my husband's death. I was fatigued and this book reminded me that is to be expected - that emotions cycle through occasionally, without warning, for years after a loss. It was what I needed to hear, delivered in a kind and upbeat tone. I will keep this wonderful resource handy for years to come.

— Kelli Reynolds, bereaved spouse,
Director of Communications, Office of the
Provost, Texas A&M University

I have been widowed for 5 1/2 years. *Heartbroken* touched on every emotion I have experienced in that time. Gary has a way of taking a very hard subject and bringing it to a level I can identify with.

— Leslie Gillespie, bereaved spouse,
Regional Director, Curo Health Services

Do you find yourself telling others, "My husband (or wife) died recently…" just to hear it again and try to believe it? Does grief still take your breath away at times? Do you wonder how ANYONE really survives such a loss? Many questions that you may have are answered in **Heartbroken** on single, easy to read pages.

— Lois Wynn, bereaved spouse

Heartbroken

HEALING FROM THE
LOSS OF A SPOUSE

REVISED AND EXPANDED EDITION

GARY ROE

OTHER BOOKS BY GARY ROE

Grief Walk: Experiencing God After the Loss of a Loved One

The Comfort Series
Comfort for Grieving Hearts: Hope and Encouragement in Times of Loss
Comfort for the Grieving Spouse's Heart: Hope and Healing After Losing Your Partner
Comfort for the Grieving Adult Child's Heart: Hope and Healing After Losing Your Parent
Comfort for the Grieving Parent's Heart: Hope and Healing After Losing Your Child

The Good Grief Series
Aftermath: Picking Up the Pieces After a Suicide
Teen Grief: Caring for the Grieving Teenage Heart
Shattered: Surviving the Loss of a Child
Please Be Patient I'm Grieving: How to Care For and Support the Grieving Heart
Surviving the Holidays Without You: Navigating Grief During Special Seasons

The Difference Maker Series
Difference Maker: Overcoming Adversity and Turning Pain into Purpose Every Day (Adult & Teen Editions)
Living on the Edge: How to Fight and Win the Battle for Your Mind and Heart (Adult & Teen Editions)

DEDICATION

Jen, this book is dedicated to you.

As a young widow, you invested heavily in your recovery and healing. And you somehow grieved well while caring for four children. You are a remarkable, amazing woman.

It's truly an honor to be married to you.

ACKNOWLEDGEMENTS

Special thanks to the bereaved spouses from Grief Support at Hospice Brazos Valley for their willingness to share their journeys. Thank you for your transparency and your desire to help others navigate this difficult valley.

Thanks to Dr. Craig Borchardt of Hospice Brazos Valley for his encouragement and support in developing this resource.

Thanks to Kathy Trim of TEAM Japan and Kelli Reynolds of Texas A&M for their English expertise and superb editing.

Thanks to Sheila Flickinger of SFCreative for her help with logo design and website management.

Thanks to Streetlight Graphics for bringing this manuscript to life with terrific design and formatting.

Thanks to all the bereaved spouses out there slogging through the quagmire of grief. You inspire me with your resiliency and courage. You're not alone.

Download your exclusive, free, printable PDF:
Healing Wisdom from Heartbroken

https://www.garyroe.com/wisdom-from-heartbroken

TABLE OF CONTENTS

INTRODUCTION

I'm sorry.

If you're reading this book, chances are you're enduring one of the greatest losses a human being can experience.

You've lost your spouse.

A UNIQUE LOSS

This death is unlike any other. She was your partner. He was your soul mate. The two of you became one. Now you feel less than whole. It seems like part of you died too.

Perhaps your marriage was strained, and now the hope for anything different is gone. Maybe regrets piled up over the years. This is a different kind of pain.

As a hospice chaplain and pastor, I've had the honor of serving hundreds of widows and widowers as they walk through this difficult and confusing valley. I've been astounded by their honesty and inspired by their courage. It's their pain, wisdom, and healing that I share with you in this book.

IN THIS BOOK...

In the following pages, you'll find over 60 readings inspired by the words and experiences of grieving widows and widowers.

Each entry...

- addresses a specific challenge bereaved spouses face
- contains an affirmation designed to encourage healthy grieving
- concludes with a related thought and inspirational quote

The readings are divided into three parts:

Part One: Managing the Emotions - addresses the raw and difficult emotions involved in your loss.

Part Two: Navigating the Relationships - focuses on your relationships and the role other people can play in your recovery and healing.

Part Three: Leaning Forward - looks at how to re-engage in life and accept your new normal.

Here's an important thing to remember: *Each reading stands on its own, so they can be tackled in any order.*

You may decide to read them sequentially. Or you might jump around, depending on what you happen to be dealing with on any given day. It's up to you. Listen to your heart.

Some entries will be more emotional than others. Some will not be easy or fun. Don't get in a hurry. Take your time. Consider keeping a journal and writing personal responses to each reading. Processing your thoughts and feelings is crucial to healthy grieving.

Each of the three main sections begins and ends with a chapter designed to help you move through your grief process. In addition, I've included some supplementary material with suggestions and resources to help you recover and heal.

THIS ISN'T EASY

Grieving is hard work. I'm glad you've decided to invest in doing it well. You're taking care of you, and that's the best thing you can do for yourself and those around you.

So, hang on. The ride may get bumpy. Move ahead at your own pace. Let the words of fellow grievers sink in and touch your heart.

You're not crazy, and you're far from alone.

DISCLAIMER

I work as a hospice chaplain and grief specialist. I am not a Licensed Professional Counselor and none of my content is meant to diagnose or treat any disease or disorder.

PART ONE:
MANAGING THE EMOTIONS

Grieving is the natural way of working
through the loss of a love.
Grieving is not weakness nor absence of faith.
Grieving is as natural as crying when you
are hurt, sleeping when you are tired or
sneezing when your nose itches.
It is nature's way of healing a broken heart.

— Doug Manning

1

THOSE CRAZY EMOTIONS

"When did they offer the roller-coaster training? Somehow I missed that."

— Sally, a hospice patient

Grief does strange things to us. It pummels our hearts and rattles
our souls. It's confusing and unnerving. We can be shocked by its
depth and power, especially when we lose a spouse.

To say that our emotions are stirred by our partner's death is a
gross understatement. Our feelings hijack us and threaten to take
over our entire existence. It's a rough and unpredictable ride. Like
hospice patient Sally above, most of us are ill-equipped for the on-
slaught of this emotional roller-coaster.

THE NORMAL BALANCE OF REASON
AND EMOTION IS GONE

Human beings are both emotional and rational beings. Some of us
operate more on emotion, while others trust more in reason. Which
one tends to dominate and how much depends on a variety of fac-
tors like background, experience, gifts, talents, and personality. Each
of us has a natural sort of equilibrium, a balance of emotion and
reason that we settle into in the midst of routine, everyday life.

When grief strikes, this equilibrium is upended. Our usual balance of emotion-reason cracks under the strain. The heart exerts
itself, and emotion floods our being.

As Sam put it, "I never knew I was capable of feeling such things. I'm suddenly an emotional basket case. I'm not myself at all."

The truth is, Sam was still himself, but he was in a very different situation. Something traumatic occurred. His wife died. Powerful emotions surged forth from deep within him. Because his feelings took up a lot more space than usual, his reason naturally got squeezed into the backseat.

In other words, having roller-coaster emotions during this time is *normal*.

UP, DOWN, AND ALL AROUND

"How am I doing? Up, down, and all around. My emotions are all over the map," Sandra shared.

Grief emotions come in all shapes and sizes, ranging from mild to severe:

- Shock, numbness, feeling nothing
- Sadness, sorrow, depression
- Fear, dread, terror
- Irritability, anger, rage
- Nervousness, anxiety, panic

Some feelings are fairly constant, like a dull ache in the heart. They form a new atmosphere of sorrow that surrounds the death of a spouse. Others are like sudden, sharp daggers. They strike like lightning. As one widow put it, "It's like a thousand needles have been thrust into my soul."

How do you deal with this complicated quagmire of emotions?

It begins with recognizing a key truth about feelings.

A FOUNDATIONAL TRUTH ABOUT EMOTIONS

There is a foundational truth about emotions that everyone in grief (and not in grief, for that matter) needs to know: *Feelings are not facts. They are just emotions.*

In other words, your feelings are *real*, but they are not *reality.*

Here are some examples:

You might feel very alone. Are you? Yes, in the sense that your loss is unique. But in another sense, you are never alone. Many have endured the death of a spouse, and many are going through it now.

You could feel like you're going crazy or about to come unhinged. Are you? Probably not. But you are in a crazy situation compared to "normal" life. Everything has changed. No wonder you question your sanity.

You might have increased anxiety and even panic attacks. You could feel like you're going to die or the world is going to end. Anxiety is a natural reaction to loss. Your system is being hit by grief. All is not lost, and you will get through this.

Again, feelings are not facts. Emotions are real, but they are not reality.

So what do you do?

HANDLING THOSE CRAZY EMOTIONS

How do you handle these crazy emotions?

Feelings are meant to be felt. When the emotion comes, acknowledge it.

"I feel sad."

"I'm really angry right now."

"I feel so alone. I feel empty and depressed."

Simply voicing feelings out loud has tremendous value. Some people keep a "feeling journal," where they can write their emotions uncensored. Others share freely and honestly in a support group setting or with trusted friends.

As you acknowledge the emotion and feel it, you're processing what's happening in your mind and heart. You're opening yourself up to grieve well and to begin to recover and heal.

Emotions must be felt. Let them be what they are. When you do this, you honor your spouse. By taking your emotions seriously, you're telling your loved one (and yourself) how important they are to you and how much you love them.

BEWARE IMPULSIVE DECISION-MAKING

Feelings are sneaky. They can dupe you. They can come on so strong at times you'll doubt your ability to deal with them. You'll want to run.

Grief emotions can be oppressive. They can wear you down to where you might be willing to do almost anything to feel better.

That's the danger zone.

Remember the basic truth about emotions: *Feelings are not facts. They are real, but they are not reality.* Acknowledge and feel them, but don't go making major, life-changing decisions based on them.

The desire to feel better can push people to unhealthy decision-making like hasty relationships and poor financial choices. People can revert to old addictions, or pursue new ones. This time of grief is hard enough. You don't want or need a pile of regrets on top of it all to deal with later.

A counselor friend of mine says, "The only way out of the pain is through it." Grief is real. It is designed to be felt. Healthy grieving is one of the keys to healing your broken heart.

WE ALL NEED REASSURANCE

Most of us who are grieving need reassurance. Perhaps you do too. While grieving, you need to know that:

You're not alone.

You're not crazy.

You're going to be okay.

In the readings that follow, widows and widowers share with you their roller-coaster journeys in handling the crazy emotions of grief. Chances are, your heart will resonate with their words and you'll see yourself in their stories.

Emotions will surface. As they come, acknowledge and feel them.

Don't get in a hurry. Take your time.

Be nice to yourself.

Remember to breathe.

It's not that death came now,
but that it came at all.

2

"THIS CAN'T BE HAPPENING"

"This can't be happening. This isn't real. No, no, no!" Sandra said, as she laid her head next to her husband's.

Mark had just passed of pancreatic cancer. He had done well for a while, and then suddenly declined. Sandra and the rest of the family had been shocked by the speed of it all.

"No. You can't be gone. You just can't be gone," she whispered.

You knew this was going to happen someday. You understood that most likely one of you would be left behind. But when the day of separation came, it felt wrong somehow. You were meant to be together. Forever.

And now, there is this shocking emptiness.

It's not just that death came now, but that it came at all.

"I don't want this to be real. I love you. I must breathe."

———— ◆ ————

Shock is our first response to loss.

It's natural, and it's designed to protect our hearts.

3

"I'M STUNNED"

Steve sat on a park bench, staring at the trees in the distance.

"I'm stunned," he said with a sigh.

Steve's wife Jennifer had just died of breast cancer. She'd been fighting the disease for years and had finally succumbed. Steve had hardly uttered a word since.

"I'm just stunned," he repeated.

It feels like you've been punched in the gut or hit by a large truck. You're in a daze. Life seems to be moving in slow motion. Someone pushed the pause button on your heart.

But it's more than that. Perhaps this is worse than anything else that has happened to you.

Of course you're stunned. How could you not be? Your partner is gone.

"I'm stunned. I should be. I'll breathe
deeply and be kind to myself."

Grief is like an emotional concussion.

It leaves us stunned and shaken.

"When one person is missing the
whole world seems empty."

— Pat Schweibert,
Tear Soup: A Recipe for Healing After Loss

4

"THE FUNERAL IS OVER, BUT THE LOSS ISN'T"

"I'm glad that's done," Rebecca sighed as she climbed into the car. "The service was wonderful. It honored Rick in every way."

Rebecca sighed again before continuing. "The funeral is over, but the loss isn't."

Rebecca was right. The loss is permanent. Rick cannot be replaced. He occupied a unique space on the planet and in Rebecca's heart.

The memorial service may be over, but your grief isn't. Not by a long shot. And everything counts: memorial services, anniversaries, and birthdays; candles lit, letters written, and balloons released; memories shared, photos posted, and stories composed. These add up, and help heal your heart over time.

This isn't a sprint, but a marathon. Pace yourself. Take your heart seriously. Breathe.

"Grief is a marathon. I'll remember
you, and pace myself well."

⬥

Grief has its own timetable.

It's different for each person.

Grief will not be rushed.

5

"MY HEART IS BROKEN"

"My man is gone, and my heart is broken," Cassandra said.

Cassandra's husband Marty had been dead several days. His memorial service was about to begin, and she was bracing herself to enter the chapel.

"I don't want to do this," she said. Then she turned and locked eyes with me. "It's true what they say – that you don't know what you've got till it's gone," she continued.

When you married, two hearts became one. Your hearts became deeply intertwined. You did life together as intimate partners.

Then death came.

How can two-hearts-become-one be separated again? How can you let go of what has become your own heart?

No wonder this hurts. Your heart has been torn. The pain is real.

***"My heart is torn because it is one
with yours. This is painful."***

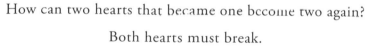

How can two hearts that became one become two again?

Both hearts must break.

This is the painful side of love.

"The LORD is close to the brokenhearted and
saves those who are crushed in spirit."

— Psalm 34:18

FOR REFLECTION AND/ OR JOURNALING

"If I were to make a list of words describing how I've felt since losing my spouse, I would say…"

_____

_____

_____

_____

_____

_____

_____

_____

_____

_____

_____

_____

6

"I'M LEARNING TO EXPRESS WHAT I'M FEELING"

"I'm slow at this grief thing. I'm learning to express what I'm feeling. Sharing what I'm going through isn't natural for me," Art said.

"I'm not good at it, but I'm trying," he continued, smiling.

All of us live using a unique combination of logic and emotion. You may normally operate more in one realm than the other. When in grief, however, emotion begins to take over. No matter who we are, logic tends to get squeezed into a corner.

Expressing what you're feeling is important. Some keep a journal. Others speak it out loud. Still others write letters to their deceased spouses.

It's surprising how powerful a simple statement of emotion like "I feel sad" or "I feel angry" can be. Pay attention to your feelings. Your heart is worth it.

> *"I'll learn to pay attention to what I'm feeling. This is part of honoring you."*

He that conceals his grief finds no remedy for it.

— Turkish Proverb

7

"IT WAS ALL SO SUDDEN"

"It happened so quickly. One minute he seemed fine, and the next he was gone. It was all so sudden," Connie said through her tears.

Matt had been mowing the lawn. He came inside, sat down in his recliner and fell asleep.

He never woke up.

Connie's eyes showed she was still in shock. She couldn't wrap her mind around what had happened, much less her heart.

Sudden death comes with unique challenges. You didn't see it coming. It took you by surprise. There was no final, "I love you." You didn't get to say goodbye.

How could you not feel unfinished? Things were left unsaid and undone. You wonder *"What if..."* and *"If only..."*

Your heart is searching for solid rock in the midst of this free fall. He was just here. How could he be gone?

"You were just here. How could you be gone?"

Life can be gone in an instant.

When it departs, the shock waves are immense.

"It is possible to provide security against other ills, but as far as death is concerned, we men live in a city without walls."

— Epicurus

8

"I CAN'T CATCH
MY BREATH"

"It's constant. I had no idea how hard it would be. The depth of the grief is astounding," Maggie shared.

"Sometimes I feel like I can't even catch my breath."

Grief carries a powerful punch. It slams us emotionally, mentally, and physically. We forget things. We become suddenly clumsy. Our immune system can be compromised. We get sick more often.

Perhaps you literally can't catch your breath. Hyperventilation is a natural result of the anxiety that accompanies a large loss. Grief pounds your entire system and affects your whole person.

Chances are you're surprised by how constant, hard, and deep your grief is. All of this honors your spouse and your relationship. Grieving well is not for sissies. It takes serious courage.

It may not feel like it, but you are more courageous than you know.

*"My grief is deeper than I imagined, but
I can meet it with courage today."*

⬅◈➡

Courage isn't the absence of fear, but the willingness
to feel the fear and not be controlled by it.

"No one ever told me that grief felt so like fear."

— C. S. Lewis, *A Grief Observed*

9
"I THOUGHT I WAS PREPARED"

"We've known for years it was coming. I thought I was prepared. I guess not," Sam exclaimed, tears streaming down his face.

Maggie, Sam's wife, had been gone for a couple of months. All their paperwork was in order well in advance, and her funeral arrangements were completed beforehand. Sam was a planner, but nothing could prepare him for life without Maggie.

"I get surprised every day by her absence. Nope, there was no way I could prepare for this," he continued.

Nothing could completely prepare you for incredible impact of your loss. Your hearts were one. You did life together. Your spouse's absence affects everything.

I mean everything.

Grief is a long and winding road with many twists and turns. Expect the unexpected. Be patient with yourself.

"Nothing could prepare me for losing you.
I feel your absence everywhere."

———◆———

In the end, grief surprises us.
Nothing can fully prepare the heart for it.

10
"THIS HURTS SO BADLY"

"This hurts so badly! It's like someone is putting my guts through a meat grinder. I'm getting chewed up from the inside out," Bruce confided.

"When I go out, I fake it. I smile, but the truth is my heart is crushed."

The pain can be excruciating. When you married, you became one with your spouse. How can one be divided without deep, soul-wrenching anguish?

It can be painful beyond description. You may feel numb simply because you can't process the depth of the agony.

You can put a good face on it, but you won't be able to maintain it long. As you learn to be real with your own heart about the pain, you will begin to heal. If you make the courageous choice to feel your emotions, you'll grow. You'll also appreciate your loved one even more.

It's okay to hurt. How could you not?

> *"The pain is astounding. How could*
> *it not be? I love you."*

As we allow ourselves to feel the pain,
our hearts will begin to heal.

"I am feeble and utterly crushed; I
groan in anguish of heart."

— Psalm 38:8

FOR REFLECTION AND/ OR JOURNALING

"When I think of my loss, I have many questions. For example..."

_____

_____

_____

_____

_____

_____

_____

_____

_____

_____

_____

_____

11

"I'M NUMB"

"I'm just here. I don't feel anything," Sam said, staring out his living room window. "The world is still out there, but I'm not interested. It doesn't seem to matter what I do or where I go. I'm going through the motions."

Sam paused and turned toward me.

"I'm numb," he whispered.

Numb. One definition reads, "deprived of the power to feel; emotionally unresponsive, indifferent."

You've been hit and are suffering a sort of emotional concussion. Life becomes foggy. Fatigue comes in waves. You move in a daze.

The color has gone. Everything is a dull grey.

What happened? Where did she go? Why did he leave? What now?

The questions swirl in your traumatized heart. No wonder you're numb.

Breathe. This is a part of grief.

"I'm numb. Where did you go? I love you."

<hr />

Your heart has been traumatized.

How could you not be numb?

12

"I'M ANXIOUS ABOUT EVERYTHING"

"I'm having trouble sleeping. My mind won't settle. I'm nervous and fidgety. I can't concentrate," Mary said, gently rocking back and forth.

"I seem to be anxious about everything."

Anxiety often accompanies grief. Even normally calm individuals have their share of anxious moments during the loss of a spouse.

Everything is changing. You're grieving what you lost. You're wondering what to do. You don't know what's ahead. You've never been here before. Having some anxiety is natural.

Grief initiates a fight-or-flight response. Your brain interprets you're in danger, and it acts to protect you. Anxiety preps you to do battle or to run.

Give yourself a break. If you're expecting to sail through this, that's not realistic. You'll get anxious, and that's okay.

Be nice to you. Your loved one would want that.

> *"I may get anxious, but that doesn't*
> *mean I'm in danger. It will pass."*

If you're experiencing panic attacks and anxiety is impairing your life, *it's time to seek professional help.*

Contact your medical doctor or a mental health professional

(the best route may be to involve both). They'll help you devise a plan for managing your emotions during this time.

Needing help isn't weakness. Seeking assistance when you need it is courageous and wise.

13
"I'M TIRED ALL THE TIME"

"I don't know what's happening. I'm tired all the time. I'm exhausted. It's so bad, I don't even want to chew," Brenda said.

"Seriously, I'm barely functioning. And I get sick a lot. Grief runs deeper than I thought."

Grief requires an astounding amount of energy. Don't expect things to be routine. They won't be. Life will be a whole new ballgame for a while.

Grief is exhausting. It suppresses the immune system and deadens the appetite. Your body feels the stress and shifts into survival mode. Sleep is often disturbed and memory becomes temporarily impaired.

Your body is sending you messages. Grief is hard and demanding. Take it seriously. Slow down. Don't expect as much. Eat well. Exercise. Honor your spouse by taking care of yourself.

The fatigue is real. Rest.

"Grief is exhausting. I'll honor you by taking care of me."

———◈———

Grief requires an astounding amount of energy.

"I am worn out from my groaning. All night long I flood
my bed with weeping and drench my couch with tears."

— Psalm 6:6

14

"THE AIR I BREATHE
IS A REMINDER"

"I long for her touch. I miss holding hands. I miss her voice. I miss her presence next to me in the bed. Nights last forever," Pete shared, his eyes closed and his lips trembling.

He sniffled, and looked into my eyes.

"She's everywhere and nowhere. The air I breathe is a reminder," he said.

Your spouse is everywhere. She's the atmosphere of your home, and your life. The very air you breathe can be a reminder of her absence.

It's hard to escape the atmosphere you exist in. In fact, it's impossible. You've breathed her in for so long, your mind says she's still here – and your heart longs to believe it.

Then it hits. She's gone. But you still need to breathe.

Every breath can seem labored. Grief is everywhere. Her absence is like a lack of oxygen.

Perhaps you search for her. You miss her badly.

"You were the air I breathed. Your
absence is like a lack of oxygen."

"Without you in my arms, I feel an
emptiness in my soul. I find myself searching
the crowds for your face – I know it's an
impossibility, but I cannot help myself."

— Nicholas Sparks, *Message in a Bottle*

15

"I'VE LOST MY BEST FRIEND"

"I've lost my best friend. How does a person recover from that?" Mary said, clinging to a photo of her late husband Mike.

"We went through a lot together. I can't imagine life without him," she continued.

You came out of the womb designed for relationship. You grew, and discovered friendship. Then you met someone you could lock hearts with. You married and had a new kind of best friend.

Your companionship was unique. You tackled life together, with all of its curves, potholes, and speed bumps. You came to understand and trust one another. It wasn't perfect, but you were in it together.

You've lost your best friend. Your heart has been shattered. And that hurts. Badly.

Your pain honors your spouse.

"You're my best friend. Life will be so different without you."

This hurts.

"Be merciful to me, LORD, for I am in distress; my eyes grow weak with sorrow, my soul and body with grief."

— Psalm 31:9

FOR REFLECTION AND/ OR JOURNALING

"Since my loss, I find I get anxious about..."

_____

_____

_____

_____

_____

_____

_____

_____

_____

_____

_____

_____

_____

16

"OUR MARRIAGE
WASN'T THE BEST"

"To be honest, our marriage wasn't the best. It was strained. We said many things both of us regretted," Samantha said.

"When Stephen died, all hope of something better was gone. It's all so, well, unsatisfying. Frankly, I feel robbed," she concluded.

No marriage is perfect. If we don't stay current on owning up to and forgiving offenses, resentments can pile up. Death can intervene and make reconciliation impossible.

If this describes your marriage, you have to somehow make peace with what happened. You not only get to grieve what you lost, but also what you wished for and never had.

Losses that aren't acknowledged and grieved well become unresolved issues that can sabotage future dreams and relationships. Don't let that happen.

You can't go back, but you can still deal with what was in your own heart. Grieving is an opportunity to make peace with the past.

"I need to grieve both what I lost and what I never had."

You can't go back, but you can still deal
with what was in your own heart.
Grieving is an opportunity to make peace with the past.
For help in dealing with the wounds of the past, check
out some of my resources at www.garyroe.com.

17
"EVERYTHING REMINDS ME OF HIM"

"What do I miss?" Andrea asked. "Everything! I miss everything. Everything reminds me of Aaron."

"It doesn't matter where I go or what I do, he's gone. And it keeps hitting me in the face over and over and over again," she continued.

Reminders are everywhere. Aromas, places, songs, and people. The list goes on and on. Anything can trigger a memory.

You're walking through an emotional mine field every moment. When and from where is the next grief wave going to come? To say this is challenging is a gross understatement.

This is incredibly exhausting. But it also declares how special your spouse was and is to you. She or he is everywhere. Of course. You were one.

Walk carefully. Breathe deeply. One mine at a time. As you grieve, you'll find yourself treasuring the memories more and more.

"Everything seems to remind me of you.
I'll learn to treasure each memory."

Reminders are everywhere.

This can be difficult, but as you grieve you'll find yourself treasuring the memories more and more.

18
"I FEEL LOST"

Cal sat at the dining table staring out the window. He sighed and even moaned from time to time. Tears tumbled down his cheeks.

"I feel lost," he said softly. "What am I going to do? How am I supposed to be? Who am I without Sarah?"

He turned and looked into my eyes. "I don't know how to do this," he said.

How could he know what to do? Cal had never been here before.

Neither have you.

Even if you've had similar losses, *this death is different.* Your spouse was one-of-a-kind. Your relationship was unique. You've suddenly been dropped into uncharted territory.

No wonder you feel lost.

It will take time to get your bearings. Be gentle with yourself. As your heart heals, answers will come.

> *"Without you, I feel lost, but answers*
> *will come as I need them."*

You're in uncharted territory.

It will take time to get your bearings.

19

"I MISS HIS VOICE"

"There's no one else like him. The intimacy we enjoyed was special. We were true partners," Betty shared.

"I especially loved all the playful, verbal bantering. It was so much fun. I even made a list of words we used in our everyday conversation."

Betty paused and sighed.

"Goodness, I miss his voice," she said.

The power of the human voice is extraordinary. Like the eyes, the voice uniquely expresses our hearts and minds. It's one of the first things many bereaved spouses say they miss.

What your mate said, and how, is deeply imbedded in your soul. His words are weighty and powerful.

His voice may be silent to your ear, but not to your heart. He still speaks to you. His words linger. Treasure them.

"I miss your voice, but I hear it deep
inside. I'll treasure your words."

The power of the human voice is extraordinary.

His voice may be silent to your ear, but not to your heart.

20

"AM I GOING CRAZY?"

"I'm forgetting things. My keys. Appointments. What I came into the room for. What I just said," Wes shared.

"I can't think straight. I feel kind of looney. Am I going crazy?" he asked.

No, Wes wasn't crazy. Neither are you. But you are in a crazy situation.

You've lost your spouse. Your right arm is gone. You're heart has been torn in two. You feel like a half-person now.

Dreams are broken. Plans are shattered. What you counted on is no longer. Everything has changed.

It's like a sinkhole opened up beneath you and you're in a free fall to who knows where. You're dazed and drained. Life is surreal. Emotional pain greets you around every corner.

Things are different, even crazy right now. No wonder you don't feel like yourself. It's not you. It's grief.

"I'm not crazy, but life without you is."

———◆———

You're not crazy.

You're in a crazy situation.

"I am bowed down and brought very low;
all day long I go about mourning."

— Psalm 38:6

FOR REFLECTION AND/ OR JOURNALING

"Since losing my spouse, I find myself missing many things. For example..."

_____

_____

_____

_____

_____

_____

_____

_____

_____

_____

_____

21
"I FEEL GUILTY"

"I feel so guilty. Ronnie and I had a fight before he passed, and I never apologized. I didn't tell him I loved him that night either," Barb said.

"And that's just the beginning. There's so much I wanted to say to him, but never did," she continued.

Regrets have incredible power. They can quickly ravage your heart.

Guilt is sneaky. It tries to trick you into living in the realm of *what-if* and *if-only*. Once you engage with guilt, life can turn into an emotional treadmill from which it is difficult to step off.

Yet, regrets are real, and you must deal with them.

Own up to what's yours. Ask forgiveness. Just hearing yourself say it out loud will have an impact.

Then do the hardest thing: forgive yourself. And when guilt comes knocking, send it packing.

> *"I'll honor you by forgiving myself for
> what I did and didn't do."*

———<—>———

Forgive.

Ask forgiveness.

Forgive yourself.

Send guilt packing.

"Guilt is perhaps the most painful
companion to death."

— Elisabeth Kübler-Ross

22
"I'M RELIEVED"

"Believe it or not, I'm relieved. I'm glad it's over. He didn't want to live that way, and now he's at peace. He's not suffering anymore," Caroline said.

Caroline's husband Randy suffered from ALS. He lost muscle control until finally all he could do was move his eyes. His mind, however, was incredibly sharp. He was a man trapped inside his own body.

Some diseases are especially cruel. They steal our most precious abilities. They rob us slowly and methodically.

If you watched your mate suffer, how could you not feel some relief? You felt his pain, and were powerless to do anything about it. You fought alongside him in this long and weary conflict.

Perhaps the relief you are feeling now is his.

"I miss you, but I'm relieved you're
not suffering anymore."

———◆———

Watching a mate suffer is excruciating.

Feeling relieved when it's over is natural.

Perhaps the relief you feel now is his.

23

"WHY?"

"I don't understand. Why do people have to die? Why did this happen? Why her? Why us? Why now?" John cried, with his head in his hands.

John's wife Janet had died several days prior of lung cancer. Since she had never smoked, John saw the whole situation as some cruel joke. It shouldn't have happened.

But it did.

We have trouble when things don't make sense. The difficulty is that life is often unpredictable and confusing. Our hearts struggle when something precious is taken from us, especially a loved one. Especially a spouse.

Why did it have to happen? Why to her? Why to him? Why to you? Why now? Why?

Your heart needs to be free to grapple with these questions.

"I'll take the questions of my heart seriously, including 'Why?'"

"Why?" often has no answers; yet our wounded hearts must still ask the question.

24

"I HATE COMING HOME TO AN EMPTY HOUSE"

"I hate coming home to an empty house. I always expect to hear her welcoming me home, and the silence shocks me," Andy said.

"I remember waking up one morning and it hit me, hard. I'm a widower. I'm alone. Weekends are the worst," he continued.

Home has changed. Your spouse's absence is palpable. It's like her voice resonates in the air, without being heard. The silence can indeed be deafening.

Even if you have kids at home, you're keenly aware of who's missing. Your mate's absence greets you at the door, in the kitchen, around every corner, and in the bedroom.

The emptiness can overwhelm you. The house may not feel like home anymore.

Yes, sometimes things can be too quiet.

> *"It hurts that I can no longer come home to*
> *you. I feel your absence everywhere."*

The silence can be shocking.

Absence greets us everywhere.

25

"I MISS THE LITTLE THINGS"

"Everything reminds me that Craig is gone. I especially miss the little things," Selena said as she stood in her kitchen.

"He opened the door for me. He put gas in the lawnmower. He grilled. He hogged the remote. He took out the trash."

She glanced at a pickle jar on the counter. "There's no one to open jars for me now," she said.

The little things are more important than we realize.

Perhaps your mind is filling now with some of the little things your spouse did – those endearing, even frustrating quirks that were part of his or her personality.

Reminders will bring tears. Further down the road, they'll also bring smiles and laughter.

Go ahead and miss the little things. Life is comprised of them. They matter more than you know.

"I'll cherish the little things I miss about you. I never want to forget them."

"There's no one to open jars for me now."

— Selena, a widow

"You care so much you feel as though you will bleed to death with the pain of it."

— J.K. Rowling,
Harry Potter and the Order of the Phoenix

FOR REFLECTION AND/ OR JOURNALING

"Looking back, I wish I had..."

_____

_____

_____

_____

_____

_____

_____

_____

_____

_____

_____

_____

_____

26

"I DIDN'T KNOW
WHAT I HAD"

"I should've been happier. Life is too short not to be happy. You never know what's around the corner," Marty said, staring at the floor.

"I took her for granted. I didn't know what I had."

It seems that taking people and things for granted is part of being human. We get used to blessings, and they become routine to us. And the greatest gifts are people, especially our spouses.

When people are taken from us, we feel the gigantic hole they leave. We comprehend more deeply their importance. Guilt again knocks on our door.

Perhaps you feel you took your spouse for granted. Maybe you wish you had expressed more appreciation, love, and admiration.

This is part of the process – grieving what you did or didn't do, feeling the remorse, and forgiving yourself.

It would have been impossible for you to appreciate her full value. Only God knows her true worth. Be thankful for her today.

"I'm sorry I took you for granted. Please forgive me. I'm so thankful for you."

———◇———

The greatest gifts we have are people.
Especially our spouses.

27

"I THROW EGGS AND BREAK DISHES"

"I was mad! I didn't want to believe or accept it. How dare he leave me? How dare anyone take him from me?" Theresa said.

"So, I began throwing eggs and breaking dishes. I went through ten dishes. I felt better. By the time I got to the fifth egg, I was laughing," she continued, smiling.

Anger is a part of grief. It's real, and it's powerful.

Anger pushes on our hearts from the inside. If we don't express it well, it may leak out later in ways we'll regret.

A chunk of you is gone. How could you not be angry? Your anger is saying you loved them and they mattered.

Anger is natural and normal. Take care of yourself by finding healthy ways to let it out.

Try some eggs and dishes.

"When I feel angry, I'll honor you by expressing it well."

Anger pushes on the heart from the inside. It will be expressed.
Better to do it in a healthy manner than for it to leak out in less beneficial ways.

28
"I LOST HIM IN PIECES"

"Thank goodness that's over!" Ruth exclaimed. "I feel so relieved, but also empty."

"I've been losing him for years with this disease. One piece at a time. One brain pathway at a time. It was awful," she said.

Alzheimer's, dementia, and other degenerative diseases are especially taxing. You lose your spouse one memory at a time. It can seem like your mate died a long time ago, and all that's left is a shell.

This kind of death can come with a great amount of relief. He's not suffering anymore. But it can also feel hollow and unsatisfying because of the lack of closure in many areas.

Like the diseases themselves, the grief that follows can be confusing and complicated. Your grief may be a bit like a maze.

Don't go it alone. With help, you'll find your way through it.

*"I lost him slowly and in pieces. No wonder
my grief feels so fragmented."*

⟨———⟩

If a degenerative disease was involved, perhaps you
lost your spouse in stages – one piece at a time.
You grieve the same way.
One day at a time.
Others can help in this process, especially those who
know grief and have been through a similar valley.
Don't go it alone.

29

"IT'S NOT FAIR!"

"It's not fair. When I leave the house, I see couples everywhere – holding hands, having dinner, laughing, talking. It drives me crazy," Lori said.

"It's just not fair!" she exclaimed.

No, it's not.

Seeing other couples, even in a movie, may set you off. It reminds you of what you've lost and the pain comes cascading in.

How dare someone else be happy! You've lost your mate!

The world can be callous and indifferent to your loss. It goes on spinning, even though your life seems to have been placed on hold. It's no wonder you sometimes feel alone in your grief.

It's not fair. It hurts.

Anger would be a natural result, along with some extreme sadness and disappointment. It's okay to have these feelings. These emotions are natural, and can honor your spouse.

> *"When things feel unfair, I'll focus*
> *on you and on grieving well."*

———♦———

It's not fair.

"My eyes have grown dim with grief;
my whole frame is but a shadow."

— Job 17:7

30
"I FEEL DEPRESSED"

"I have no motivation. I don't want to do anything. Nothing sounds good. I manage to get out of bed, but I don't want to," Tamara shared in a pained whisper.

She sighed, and looked out her living room window.

"I can't go any of the usual places. It's like all joy evaporated. I feel depressed," she said.

Depression is a natural part of grief. When the reality of your loss sinks in, things can grow dark. Joy is elusive. Fun is nowhere to be found.

You might experience some extreme sadness, lack of motivation, and general disinterest in life. You could find yourself pulling back relationally and wanting to hide.

This is natural. You've been severely wounded. You need time and space to recover.

Breathe deeply. Be nice to you. Allow your heart to heal.

"I may experience some depression.
This is natural. I miss you."

Normal depression during this time can keep you down for a day or two, but doesn't control all of life.

You still get out, function, and carry on some daily activities.

If this withdrawal and general disinterest become constant and continue for more than two weeks, it's time to seek professional help.

See your medical and mental health professional immediately.

FOR REFLECTION AND/ OR JOURNALING

"Since losing my spouse, I find myself wondering about..."

_____

_____

_____

_____

_____

_____

_____

_____

_____

_____

_____

_____

_____

31

"SHE DIDN'T
DESERVE THIS"

"I can't believe this! How could this happen? She was a virtual angel. All she did was love and serve people!" David yelled.

"She didn't deserve this! Our family didn't deserve this! This is all wrong!" he ranted, pacing around his living room.

Life is tough enough. It's stocked with challenges from birth. Tragedies happen. So much doesn't make sense.

Perhaps you're angry. You may question things you thought were rock solid, like your faith, God, or the goodness of other people. You may doubt your own sanity.

Punch the pillow. Scream in the car. Write it out. Rant to a safe person. Find positive ways to express this powerful emotion.

Yes, it feels wrong. You might feel robbed or cheated somehow. You miss your partner. How could you not be upset?

Be honest with your own heart.

*"Losing you feels wrong. I'll find positive
ways to express my anger."*

Anger is a powerful, natural part of grief.
We need to be honest with our own hearts.

"Grief teaches the steadiest minds to waver."

— Sophocles, *Antigone*

32
"EVERYTHING THAT HAPPENS IS BIG NOW"

"Everything that happens is big now. Every little issue is magnified, because I'm by myself," Tiffany shared, wringing the napkin in her hands.

"I get sad and mad at the same time. Why am I having to do his job?"

There were two of you. Now there's one. That means everything falls on you.

More paperwork arrives. Bills come. People are calling. The house is screaming for attention. There's work to do. Your to-do list is a mile long.

You wonder how you're going to do it all. It seems unfair. You're already exhausted. Grief is draining. Can't you just mourn in peace?

Even the smallest issues now feel gigantic.

How are you going to do this?

Your number one priority is to grieve – and to do it well. Everything else will follow naturally behind.

> *"Even little things seem huge without you. Grief can be overwhelming."*

⊰◈⊱

Grief can make the smallest issues seem gigantic.
That makes sense.
There's only one of you now.

33

"LIFE AS I KNEW IT IS DONE"

"It's over. Life as I knew it is done," William said.

William's wife Mona had recently died after a protracted battle with congestive heart failure. She had struggled to breathe for years, and part of William was glad to see her suffering end.

Mona was his life. He was her caregiver during those years and had walked through her disease with her. The illness brought them closer together than ever.

Now she was gone. William felt cut adrift and even purposeless.

When you married, you became one with your spouse in many ways. Every part of life was connected to them somehow. Things are different now.

Your life has changed forever. Nothing will be quite the same ever again. How could it be? You might even wonder why you're here.

Yes, your spouse was that special.

"My life has changed forever. You're that special to me."

"You will be whole again but you will never be the same.

Nor should you be the same nor would you want to."

— Elisabeth Kübler-Ross

34

"MY DREAMS ARE GONE"

"My dreams are gone. Anything I thought I wanted to do disappeared. The goals are no more. It was all tied to him," Renee said.

"I miss the future – our future. It's not there anymore," she shared.

When your spouse passed, your future turned upside down. Anything you had planned together has been erased. Dreams, hopes, and goals died with him.

Grief is an earthquake in the heart. The aftershocks continue. You'll be experiencing them for a while. Life may feel shaky and uncertain.

Now you're faced with not only huge loss, but massive rebuilding. That won't happen quickly. Don't get in a hurry. This isn't a sprint.

As you focus on grieving well, you'll be able later to handle the challenges of remaking the future – one step at a time.

My dreams are shattered. I'll grieve in healthy ways and retool the future when it's time."

"For I know the plans I have for you," declares
the LORD, "Plans to prosper you and not to harm
you, plans to give you hope and a future."

— Jeremiah 29:11

35
"I CAN'T IMAGINE THE WORLD WITHOUT HER"

"She was the most wonderful woman. Words can't express how much I loved her. She's gone, and now there's a hole where my heart was," Larry said, staring at his wife Darlene's picture.

"I can't imagine a world without her. She was my life. What am I supposed to do now? How am I going to go on living?"

When a spouse dies, our lives change instantly. Everything is impacted. Life as we've known it is over.

You're feeling the pain of this great loss and its incredible impact. Like a tsunami, it sweeps over everything. Grief carries you along in its wake. Life becomes about survival.

You don't know what life will be like now. It's hard, if not impossible, to contemplate. You can't see around this bend in the road. But as you live one-day-at-a-time, the path ahead will become visible.

For now, focus on the next step.

"I can't imagine life without you, but somehow I'll find a way to live with even greater meaning and purpose."

⟵——◈——⟶

If you're thinking that life is no longer worth living, please reach out for help.

Contact someone you trust and seek the assistance of a mental health professional immediately.

If you're thinking of harming yourself, or have a plan to do so, call 911 now.

Honor your mate and love those around you by getting the help you need today.

FOR REFLECTION AND/ OR JOURNALING

"If I were to list some of what's different since my loss, I would say..."

_____

_____

_____

_____

_____

_____

_____

_____

_____

_____

_____

36
"HALF MY HEART IS GONE"

"I'm devastated. Half my heart is gone. How does a man live with half a heart?" Robert asked.

"We had tornadoes growing up. One time we were hit hard. I remember the shock afterwards. Debris everywhere. Our home was gone. Just like that."

Robert paused and looked at me. "She was my home. Now she's gone – just like that," he said, snapping his fingers.

No matter how much time you had to prepare, you may still have that gone-just-like-that feeling. When your spouse took her last breath, your life was forever altered. The air from that final breath silently reverberated throughout your being.

The emotional debris is everywhere. Half your heart is gone. Your home has been swept away. How do you go on? How are you going to rebuild?

As you grieve, the answers will come in their proper time.

"It's okay if I feel devastated. You were my home."

❖

"You will not 'get over' the loss of a loved
one; you will learn to live with it.
You will heal and you will rebuild yourself
around the loss you have suffered."

— Elisabeth Kübler-Ross

37
"IT'S NOT GETTING
ANY EASIER"

"This isn't what I expected. It's not getting any easier. In fact, the longer it goes, the harder things seem," Marlene said.

"I had no idea what I was facing. The reality of Carl's death is setting in over time. It gets heavier every day."

Once you begin to grieve, it's surprising how deep it can go. As time goes on, the extent of your loss begins to sink in. Your spouse was connected to everything in your existence. You're not enduring just one, but a multitude of losses.

This is why many run from grief. They stuff their emotions and self-medicate. But this only harms them and their relationships.

Grief is real and must be felt. It demands our attention.

Take a moment and look to your heart. Notice what's there. Acknowledge the emotions.

One of the great lessons of grief is that life can only be lived one moment at a time.

*"Everything feels so heavy. You mean
even more to me than I knew."*

———— ◆ ————

"(Grief) is an emotional, physical and spiritual
necessity, the price you pay for love.
The only cure for grief is to grieve."

— Earl Grollman

38
RIDING THE ROLLER-COASTER WELL

"Part of living is feeling the bad stuff. If you don't, it becomes an emotional cancer that slowly eats your soul."

— Angie Kasper, Licensed Professional Counselor

That was quite a journey.

You've just traversed three dozen readings from fellow widows and widowers on managing the roller-coaster emotions of grief. Chances are you connected deeply with many of their stories. Hopefully, you can now say with a little more confidence:

"I'm not alone (though I might feel alone at times)."

"I'm not crazy (though my mind and heart might be spinning)."

"I'm going to be okay (though I don't really know what that means yet)."

As my friend Angie says above, "Part of living is feeling the bad stuff." Grief can feel bad. Awful. If we refuse to take our hearts seriously and stuff the feelings, our emotions will eventually eat us up from the inside out.

Grief might feel bad, but it can be good. It can be healing. You've lost a spouse. To grieve, and to grieve heavily, is natural. Grieving becomes the process of mending your broken heart. You learn how to love and honor your spouse in new ways.

CURRENT GRIEF TRIGGERS PAST GRIEF

You may have noticed something else while reading Part One. Your current grief may have triggered older, perhaps still unresolved pain from the past. In other words, losing your spouse can trigger emotions tied to other losses you have endured along the way.

As you read, perhaps your mind went back to other loved ones you've lost. Some people describe this as "sadness breeding sadness." The loss of a spouse can open a sort of Pandora's Box of grief. Painful memories from other deaths and traumas come spilling out, cascading down upon you.

How you process and heal from the death of your spouse will be influenced by your personal history of loss. For example:

- If you've had other major losses recently, you'll need to be especially nice to yourself. Recovery from multiple, serious wounds takes time.
- If you've dealt well with losses in the past, your track record will benefit you now. Your heart will naturally apply what has been healing for you in the past.
- If this is your first major loss, your heart is new to the grief roller-coaster. You're truly finding your way through virgin territory. Be patient, and draw deeply from the experience of others.
- If you haven't grieved well in the past, this is an opportunity to go back and work through emotional baggage. This a chance to heal old wounds as well as new ones.

What is your history of loss? How is it affecting you now?

TAKE YOUR HEART SERIOUSLY

Your heart matters. Deeply.

I believe we all have a unique purpose. We were placed here for a reason. We were designed for impact – to contribute and make a difference. The condition of our hearts can either propel us toward our mission or distract us from it.

The heart is the control center of our lives.

As King Solomon put it, *"Above all else, guard your heart; it is the spring from which everything else flows."*

Make the condition of your heart the priority of your life. It determines everything else.

You're hurting. In some senses, your heart has been broken. To grieve well and heal, you must take your own heart seriously.

How do you do that while grieving?

Be nice to yourself.

Don't get in a hurry. Take your time.

Acknowledge and feel the emotions as they come.

Don't forget to breathe.

MAKING GRIEVING WELL A PRIORITY

Our hearts define who we are, and what's in there tends to find its way out – one way or another. As you acknowledge and feel your emotions, you'll be guarding your heart and helping yourself heal.

Grief knocks on your heart from the inside. It wants out. The emotions are powerful, but if you're willing, you can navigate them well.

Be honest with your own heart.

Stay present and in the now as much as possible.

Make grieving well a high priority.

Do you need more additional grief support?
Check out our resources on www.garyroe.com.
We're here to help.

THOUGHT QUESTIONS:

How did Part One affect you? Which readings struck you the most?

Consider your personal history of loss. What losses have you experienced along the way (not only deaths, but divorce, jobs, friendships, health issues, dreams, etc)? List them.

How can you see past losses influencing your current grief process?

What's the most important thing you learned from Part One?

_____

_____

_____

_____

_____

_____

_____

_____

_____

_____

_____

_____

PART TWO: NAVIGATING THE RELATIONSHIPS

"We bereaved are not alone.
We belong to the largest company in all the world—
the company of those who have known suffering."

— Helen Keller

39
PEOPLE CAN MAKE
THE DIFFERENCE

"I have heard many things like these;
you are miserable comforters, all of you!"

— Job, from the Old Testament

———◆———

The Old Testament character of Job is a favorite for those in grief. In a single day, Job lost all 10 of his children, his property, and his possessions. Later, he lost his health. Three friends heard what happened and came to comfort him.

When they arrived, they didn't recognize him. Suffering had changed his appearance. Overwhelmed by his situation, they sat with him in the dirt, speechless, for seven days.

After a week, Job spoke. His friends had apparently had enough. The pain got to them. Instead of continuing to be with and support Job, they judged and corrected him. They tried to fix him.

They were relentless. They kept after him, convinced that he had done something horrible to deserve such calamity. They made Job responsible for the deaths of his children.

No wonder Job responded the way he did: "You are miserable comforters, all of you!"

SOME PEOPLE ARE HELPFUL, SOME AREN'T

People can make all the difference in your grief process – one way or the other. Some are helpful and comforting, while others aren't. Some are loving, while others are draining and judgmental. Some are safe. Others are toxic.

Remember King Solomon's words? *"Above all else guard your heart; it is the spring from which everything else flows."* If you want to grieve well, you'll need to take your heart seriously. Part of that is making proactive choices about whom you're going to trust and share with during this time.

NOT EVERYONE IS TRUSTWORTHY

You're vulnerable right now. Whom you choose to entrust yourself to is important.

Not everyone is trustworthy. Not everyone has the ability to handle pain and grief. Not everyone has a compassionate and loving heart.

Some people would rather fix others than deal with their own issues. Others would prefer to judge you instead of looking at their own hearts. Some folks stand eager to give advice you haven't asked for, rather than considering why they're so driven to do so.

If someone isn't dealing well with their own pain, they're not ready to help you with yours.

WELL-MEANING PEOPLE CAN SAY
THE DUMBEST THINGS

"I can't believe what other people will say," Marvin said, shaking his head. "What are they thinking?"

Mostly, they're not thinking. They're uncomfortable with the pain, and don't know what to say.

"Oh it's all right. He's in a better place." That may be true, but you want him here, now.

"There, there. Don't cry." What are you supposed to do? Smile and be happy?

"Time heals all wounds." Since when? Besides, this hurts NOW.

"Everything is okay. You're going to do great." Maybe so, but right now this is excruciating.

The underlying message in these comments is, "Please stop grieving. I feel out of control, and that makes me feel uncomfortable."

How do you deal with these innocent, but unhelpful comments?

You could do nothing. Just smile and let it slide.

You could be honest with them. "You may be right, but I'm not there yet. This really hurts."

You might simply say, "Thanks for your concern."

Whatever you decide to do, know this: *other people will not understand your grief.* They can't. They might have endured a similar loss, but that doesn't mean they know how you feel. They don't. Your loss is yours alone. He was your husband. She was your wife. You had a unique relationship.

SOME PEOPLE SAY THE MEANEST THINGS

"I can't believe what my own family is saying. He's barely in the grave, and they're actually accusing me about what they think I did or didn't do. You'd think they'd be beside me, supporting and helping. Far from it," Sandra said, her hands on her hips.

Not everyone is well-meaning, and not all comments are innocent.

You may have heard some of the following:

"Death is a part of life. Get over it."

"Life goes on, and you need to move on."

"You're still grieving?"

"You should be over this by now."

Yes, people actually say these things, and worse.

If someone has said such things to you, I'm sorry. If you can, hear what they're really saying. It's something like this:

- "Your pain brings up my losses. It hurts. Go away."
- "I can't be around grief. It scares me. I feel out of control."
- "I'm terrified of losing my spouse. I don't want to even think about it."
- "Vulnerability is weakness. I won't let anyone hurt me again."

Most likely, unresolved hurt is at the root of most judgmental and insensitive statements. Hurt people who aren't healing can make some very cutting comments.

How do you handle this?

You could respond with your version of the words of Job: "I have heard many such things as these; you are miserable comforters, all of you!" I'm smiling as I type this. I hope you know what I mean. You could be honest about how you feel about what they've said. Just don't lower yourself to their level in the process.

You could ignore them and smile. Personally, I like this option. It leaves their comment hanging in the air. Your silence forces them to consider what they've said.

You could give them a canned response. "Thanks for your concern. I'll grieve as deeply as I can and as long as it takes. I love him that much."

In any case, the basic rule of thumb is this: *Surround yourself with people who are helpful to you in your grief process, and limit your exposure to those who aren't.*

The people who will be the most help to you are what I call *safe people.*

YOU NEED SAFE PEOPLE

Everyone needs safe people in their lives, whether they're grieving or not.

What is a safe person?

A safe person…
- Accepts you for who you are, where you are.
- Has no plans for your improvement.
- Doesn't try to fix you.
- Doesn't give advice you haven't asked for.
- Has no agenda except to walk with you in whatever you're dealing with.

Safe people have usually been through their share of pain and grief. They have trudged through difficult circumstances and been honest with their own hearts. They have done the hard work and experienced much healing. They are experienced valley-walkers.

HOW TO FIND SAFE PEOPLE

Recently, I was speaking on grief at a church. When I talked about safe people, a woman raised her hand and asked with a confused look, "Where do you find people like that?"

Everyone laughed, myself included. Many people were wondering the same thing. Safe people are rare. And if you don't know any, how do you find them?

I found myself answering the question this way: Safe people recognize other safe people. *The best way to find safe people is to become a safe person yourself.*

As you work on becoming a safe person, it's amazing how safe people will be drawn to you. Safety breeds safety. We all need safety to heal, grow, and flourish.

Becoming a safe person is one way of guarding your own heart. Finding safe people and letting them serve you will make a huge impact on your healing and recovery.

PEOPLE WILL MAKE ALL THE DIFFERENCE

If you're like most grieving people I encounter, you'll be surprised who steps up to the plate to love you during this time. Some people you counted on before may fade into the background, while others who were mere acquaintances become major players. Then there's the people you didn't know before, some of whom turn out to be key to your healing.

One thing is for sure: people will make all the difference in your grief process – one way or another.

You are more vulnerable than you realize. Healthy grieving involves making proactive choices about whom you're around:

- Surround yourself with people who help you grieve and heal.
- Limit your exposure to people who aren't helpful to you.
- Intentionally spend time with safe people.
- Work on being a safe person for others.

Now, listen to the wisdom of fellow widows and widowers and what they learned about this.

As you read, take your time. Don't get in a hurry.

Notice what you're feeling. Acknowledge the emotions.

Be nice to yourself.

And don't forget to breathe.

People can make all the difference in your
grief process, one way or the other.

40

"PEOPLE JUST DON'T GET IT"

"People just don't get it, do they?" Susan exclaimed. "I can't believe what people will say! What are they thinking?"

I know you can relate.

Perhaps you've heard some of these:

"Life goes on, and you need to move on."

"It's okay."

"Are you *still* grieving?"

"Why can't you get past this?"

Maybe they're uncomfortable with your pain. Perhaps they've got unresolved grief issues of their own. Whatever the case, what people say is usually more about them than it is about you.

You may need to avoid some people. Look for those who accept you as you are.

Forgive quickly. Seek safe people. Keep sharing.

"I will seek helpful, safe people and avoid unhelpful, judgmental voices."

"Above all else, guard your heart; it is
the wellspring of your life."

— King Solomon

Forgive quickly.
Seek safe people.
Keep sharing.

41

"MY DOG REMINDS
ME EVERY DAY"

"He lays there almost all day long every day," Carla said, nodding toward her dog Sam, who was looking through a window in the living room. "He loved Max, and would wait for him right there every day."

"Even my dog reminds me that Max isn't coming home," she said, beginning to cry.

Pets are remarkable companions. Death affects them greatly. Though their grief may be less complicated than ours, they too feel sadness and confusion.

They wait. They pine. They stop eating. They look for their master, watching and hoping. They miss their loved one.

Your pet may remind you continually of your loss. Let this be an encouragement. You're not alone. They feel it too.

"Even our pet is in mourning. We miss you."

⟢⟡⟣

Pets can be great comforters.

They grieve too.

42

"HOW DO I PARENT THROUGH THIS?"

"Answering my kids' questions is tough duty. I have answers, but they seem pretty hollow. They're hurting, and looking to me to fix it," Tess said through her tears.

"That's not fair when I'm in all this pain myself. How do I parent through this?" she asked.

Parenting. You and your spouse tackled this together. Now it's just you.

Your kids are asking questions. Or perhaps they're shutting down and not talking at all. Maybe some of them are acting out. They are reeling too. Your world as a family has changed forever.

You won't be able to do it all. Don't try. Just be with them. Your presence is powerful.

Focus on taking care of you and grieving well. This is the best gift you can give your kids right now. As time goes on, you'll learn how to grieve together.

"I can be with my kids in their grief, and still grieve well.

We can do this together."

Kids have a right to their own grief too.
It's okay that they hurt.

Don't try to fix it.
This can't be fixed.
Just be with them, and love them as best you know how.
Your presence is powerful.

43
"MY KIDS ARE HURTING"

"My kids are hurting. One is angry and acting out. Another is shut down and not talking. The third is acting like nothing happened," Rachel shared, almost frantic.

"This is too much for me. What do I do?" she asked.

Rachel was already doing the most important thing. She was reaching out for help.

You won't be able to do this alone. Just as you need good people around you to recover and heal, your kids need a support team too.

Chances are, many of the people you need are already in place. Who is most supportive of you and your family right now? Who out there knows about kids and grief?

Who are the safe people who have been placed in your life for such a time as this?

Take courage. Help is closer than you think. Consider who has been placed around you.

Reach out.

***"My kids are hurting too. I'll help them
find the support they need."***

SOURCES OF GRIEF HELP
FOR YOUR KIDS

Family and friends who are supportive or have offered to help

Co-workers or people at church who are available and want to step up

Hospices / Bereavement services who deal with children and grief

Professional Counselors or Grief Specialists

Most kids need a variety of people on their support team. Don't limit yourself to just one of the above. Different folks will fill different roles.

Don't go it alone.

Reach out.

Invest in your family's recovery and healing.

FOR REFLECTION AND/ OR JOURNALING

"Since losing my spouse, I have noticed that other people..."

44

"FAMILY HAS BEEN THE MOST COMFORTING PART"

"My family has been amazing, especially her side. If I didn't know better, I'd think they have a system about who's checking on me and when. It seems like a coordinated effort," Adam stated.

"Family has been the most comforting part of this tragedy so far," he said.

You might not have expected much from family. After all, they were hit by this grief tsunami too.

But some families have the ability to rise above themselves as individuals and handle tragedy as a team. They grieve, but they also check on and serve each other selflessly.

Now isn't the time for rivalry and competition. Grief requires love and cooperation. We need each other.

Your ache is terrible, but a little heartfelt service can ease its intensity.

"Family is so important. Rather than comparing and competing, I'll find ways to cooperate."

Though he brings grief, he will show
compassion, so great is his unfailing love.

— Lamentations 3:32

45

"FAMILY HAS BEEN A PAIN"

"It's been disappointing. You'd think a family could come together at a time like this. Not this one. They've been demanding and not comforting at all," Henry said.

"Frankly, my family has been a pain."

Not all families grieve well together.

Depending on your situation, your family may not be a reliable support system for you through this time. If not, you face several challenges:

- Protect your own heart so you're free to grieve well.
- Practice forgiving quickly.
- Refuse to hold grudges.
- Find safe, trustworthy people outside your family to help you navigate this time.

Just as some people are helpful to us in our pain, others can be toxic and potentially damaging. You get to decide what to do, how, and with whom in your grief process. Invest heavily in your recovery and healing.

"I'll forgive quickly and surround
myself with helpful influences."

≺———◆———≻

Don't allow toxic influences to add to your grief.

Guard your heart.

Forgive quickly.

Refuse to hold grudges.

Limit exposure to toxic, judgmental people.

Add safe, loving individuals to your grief recovery team.

46
"NO ONE UNDERSTANDS"

"I'm so tired of hearing junk like, 'I know what you're going through,' and, 'It will be okay.' Garbage! It's not okay, it won't be okay, and they don't understand. No one understands!" Debbie exclaimed.

No, they don't. They can't.

It wasn't their spouse that died. It was yours. Your partner. Your love. Your marriage. Your relationship.

Yours. Uniquely yours.

People may be able to sympathize and walk alongside you, but no human can fully understand your grief. It's special, and it's yours alone.

This fact might bring a sense of powerful loneliness. It can also be cause for great thanksgiving. What you had was special and was ultimately between the two of you.

This grief is deep. So is the thanksgiving.

"We were unique and special. I'm so thankful for you."

———◆———

They don't understand.

They can't.

What you had was special, unique to the two of you.

47

"I'VE BEEN SURPRISED BY KINDNESS"

"I've been surprised by kindness. The love and affection of others has been wonderful," Nick said.

"They haven't been pushy, but just made themselves available. They've made a real difference for me."

Chances are you'll be surprised by kindness too, and maybe from the least likely sources.

In order to heal, you'll need some good people walking alongside you. You need safe people – folks who have no other agenda other than to be with you in your grief as you need them.

Safe people don't try to fix your pain. They don't try to talk you out of your feelings or into any decisions. They let you grieve. They respect your privacy. They're trustworthy.

You need people like this on your healing team. They want to serve you. Please let them.

"I'll find and trust some safe people.
They'll help me recover and heal."

———◆———

Safe people don't try to fix you or the situation.

They let you grieve.

48

"I WANT TO BE ALONE SOMETIMES"

"People have been very supportive. My fridge is full. People are taking me out to coffee and meals. Someone calls me almost every day," Paul said.

"I hope I don't sound ungrateful, but I need more space. I want to be alone sometimes," he continued.

Each individual is different. Some people need more alone time than others. How about you?

Positive alone time should refresh you. It allows you to feel your emotions in private. You can rest, read, or just think and process.

Watch out for isolation, however. Isolation occurs when you withdraw and no longer engage with the world. You seclude yourself and don't get out. You deliberately avoid all contact with others. This will not serve you well or help you grieve.

Get the time alone you need, but stay connected to other people.

"I'll take the alone time I need, while being careful not to isolate myself."

———◆———

Get the alone time you need, but stay connected to others.

FOR REFLECTION AND/ OR JOURNALING

"I wish the people around me could..."

_____

_____

_____

_____

_____

_____

_____

_____

_____

_____

_____

_____

49

"MY FRIENDS EVAPORATED"

"I thought I was independent, but I was wrong. Almost all the friends John and I had were couples. Now that I'm alone, I feel out of place. They don't know what to do, and neither do I," Julie said.

"It's like my friends evaporated along with John. Just seeing couples together makes me mad. Nothing is the same. This is a lot harder than I thought it would be," she shared.

Your status has changed. Even long-term friendships can be altered. Some friends may recede into the background while new ones come to the forefront.

This was a life-changing loss. The grief seemingly invades every area of your existence. Your heart has been torn. This impacts all your relationships.

In some sense, this is collateral damage – more loss resulting from the death of your spouse. There will be gains too, but you may not see them for a while.

"My heart is torn from losing you. This naturally affects all my relationships."

<hr>

When death comes, relationships change.
At first, this feels like more loss.
Over time, you will see that new,
good things have come too.

50

"PEOPLE PUSHED ME
TO MAKE DECISIONS"

"People wanted to fix me. They pushed me to make decisions about her belongings, the house, the cars, and my future. I got mad at one point. I just lost my wife! Give me a break!" Foster shared.

"So I put my foot down and didn't make any major decisions for almost a year. I'm really glad about that," he continued.

When you're in grief, the people around you can get uncomfortable. Wanting to help, they might cross the line and try to fix your situation. They feel out of control, so they want to take action.

They can think that change is the answer. They might suggest things that require you to make major decisions at a time when you need to be focused on grieving.

You've had enough change for right now. Take your time. Wisdom will show itself at the proper moment.

"I'll listen, but not let others push me. I'll take my time making decisions."

———————————◆———————————

Take your time making decisions.

Focus on grieving well.

Wisdom is never in a hurry.

51

"BUCK UP AND
GET OVER IT?"

"People are telling me to buck up and get over it. Life goes on. Put your tough shoes on. Be strong," Paula said, with an edge in her voice.

She paused and pursed her lips. Her eyes bore into mine.

"Just how do you get over a husband? Tell me that!" she quipped.

You don't. That's impossible.

We never get over people. We learn to cope and compensate. Healing and recovery is about accepting the reality of the loss over time. But getting over your mate would mean forgetting them or somehow pretending your life together never happened.

Impossible. Plus, it doesn't honor your loved one or your marriage.

You'll never get over your spouse. But you will get through this time.

> *"I'll never get over you, but I will get*
> *through this season of grief."*

◆

You won't get over your spouse, but
you will get through this time.

"If you're going through hell, keep going."

—Winston Churchill

52

"I'M MORE VULNERABLE THAN I THOUGHT"

Several months after Tom's wife Judy died, a new lady came into his life. Tom thought she genuinely cared for him. That's what he wanted to be true, but it wasn't.

"I can't believe I was so stupid. I guess I was lonely. She fooled me, and took me for quite a bit," Tom said.

"It's hard to believe people can do that. I'm guess I'm more vulnerable than I thought," he continued, his head in his hands.

Yes, you're more vulnerable than you think.

How could you not be? You've lost your spouse. You're alone, and hurting. There is a massive void in your life. It's natural to try and fill it somehow.

Healthy grieving needs to take precedence over another relationship. You need to recover and heal in order to re-engage well. Otherwise, the new relationship will be more about your grief and your desire for things to be different than about you and the other person.

"I'm more vulnerable than I know.
I'll take my time and heal."

Wanting another relationship like
the one you lost is natural.

Trying to replace what you lost while
grieving can be dangerous.

Listen to those you trust.
Consult with people who know grief.
Take your time.
Focus on healing.
You want a new relationship to be about the two
people involved, not about alleviating your pain.

53

"OTHERS DON'T WANT TO HEAR ABOUT MY PAIN"

"I've come to a conclusion: other people don't want to hear about my pain. My friends came to the funeral and called for about a week, and then *poof*. Nothing," Bart grumbled.

"Where are they? When they don't show up, what I hear is 'we don't care,'" he said.

Many people are uncomfortable with grief. Your grief may trigger unresolved pain in their past. Rather than facing it, they choose to run.

Your friends, family, and co-workers may inundate you with support and encouragement in the days following your loss. But soon attention may slow to a trickle and then evaporate altogether. Chances are, they aren't doing this on purpose. They're immersed in their own lives and simply forget.

Everyone in this dark valley needs at least a few trusted and willing valley-walkers as companions. You do too.

> *"I don't expect everyone to understand, but I do need a few trusted allies for this fight."*

Many people are running from pain and
grief, so they may run from you too.
That's about them, not about you.

"Deposits of unfinished grief reside in more American hearts than I ever imagined."

— Robert Kavanaugh

FOR REFLECTION AND/ OR JOURNALING

"The most helpful people in my grief process have been those who..."

_____

_____

_____

_____

_____

_____

_____

_____

_____

_____

_____

54

"THEY KEPT ASKING WHAT THEY COULD DO"

"I was surprised to see how much other people miss her. They hurt, and they hurt for me. I knew they were watching me and looking out for me. They kept asking what they could do," Dale said.

"Finally, I made up some things. You should have seen them. They were so happy to serve me," he continued.

No, not everyone is helpful. Some will misunderstand, and others will judge. But there are those who love you and are eager to be in this with you. They are desperate to do something to help.

Anything you don't have to do, consider delegating to them. Their hearts are enriched by serving you. By receiving, you'll actually be helping them grieve too.

Love them by letting them love you.

"I'll let others love me. This helps all of us."

❖

Some ways others might be able to help you:

Make or deliver a meal

Make or return phone calls

Run errands

Babysit kids

Take you to a movie

What else can you think of?

55
"I NEEDED PEOPLE WHO KNEW GRIEF"

"I wasn't doing well on my own. I knew I needed to be with other people, but I felt so misunderstood. Then I went to a grief support group, and that made all the difference," Helen said.

"I needed people who knew grief. I've now made friends through this loss, and they're good ones. They're lights in my darkness," she shared with a smile.

The right people can make the grief process so much more positive and healing. Like Helen, you need people who know grief.

Where do you find these people? Check online or your local newspaper for grief support groups in your area. These are most often led or sponsored by hospices, local churches, or community service organizations.

Support groups aren't for everyone, but what does it hurt to check one out?

It could make a huge difference in your life.

"I'll find some people who know grief.
We can navigate this together."

———◆———

People who know grief can help you
navigate these rough waters.
Fellow grievers can become your lights
in the current darkness.

56

"OTHERS ARE IN THE SAME BOAT"

"I went to a support group last week. I was terrified, but I'm so glad I went. I listened to their stories and it became painfully obvious: other people are in the same boat," Cathy shared.

"You might feel like you're sinking, but there are others out there who are floundering too. It helped to be with people who are in the same battle," she said.

When we're hurt, we naturally want to withdraw. If we're not careful, a heavy loss can tempt us to go internal or isolate. We can't afford to let that happen.

Others out there are also enduring the loss of a spouse. You need them, and they need you. Just being in each other's presence can be comforting and healing.

Your heart can relax a little because you know they "get it."

"Others are feeling similar pain.
We can help each other."

<hr>

It helps to be with others who are in the same battle.

Your heart can relax around them

because you know they *get it.*

FOR REFLECTION AND/
OR JOURNALING

"I need to remember that other people..."

_____

_____

_____

_____

_____

_____

_____

_____

_____

_____

_____

_____

_____

57

WHY YOU NEED A GRIEF RECOVERY TEAM

"I thought to be strong meant handling
this on my own. Fear kept me from asking
for help, and I paid the price for it."

— Sophia, a widow

We were made for connection. Life is about relationships. Yet, because of our pain, we're tempted to make grief a solitary journey.

It was never meant to be so. We were designed to do life together, and that includes grieving.

Though this grief is uniquely yours, it's not wise to go it alone. The fact that you're reading this book suggests you already know this.

You need good people with you on this journey. You need a *Grief Recovery Team*.

TEAMS ARE DIVERSE

Like any other team, these folks have different strengths and abilities. They play different positions and have different roles.

You are a whole person, with physical, emotional, and spiritual aspects. These parts of you are interacting all the time, making you who you are. Since grief impacts all of you, you're going to need help and healing in all three areas.

This means you need a diverse team.

MY IDEAL GRIEF RECOVERY TEAM

From my own personal grief experiences, and from working with thousands of bereaved family members over the years, my ideal grief recovery team would consist of the following:

Family and friends – people who share your loss, but not at the same magnitude.

Safe people – folks who accept you where you are and want to walk alongside you. They could be any of the people listed here, or a support group that knows grief.

Medical Professional – most likely your Primary Care Physician.

Mental Health Professional – a Licensed Professional Counselor or Social Worker, who can listen and speak into your life.

Chaplain, Pastor, or Spiritual Mentor – someone who can help you tune into the spiritual aspects of this process.

Church, Civic Group, or Volunteer Organization – people who keep you involved in life and service even though you're hurting.

Online Grief Support – a wealth of info, groups, and email courses available to help you. See my Additional Resources page at the back of this book.

Do you really need all these people? Perhaps not. But it's still a good idea to know who they are and where to find them. Grief is powerful and somewhat unpredictable. It doesn't hurt to be prepared.

THE MORE GRIEVERS INVEST, THE BETTER THEY DO

From my personal and professional grief experience, I can say this with confidence: those who take their grief seriously and take advantage of a variety of support networks tend to do better. They process grief more fully and heal more completely.

Like anything else in life, we usually reap greater benefits in the areas we invest most heavily in.

Your heart is worth it. Those you love are worth it. Invest heavily in your recovery and healing.

You were never meant to grieve alone.

Do you know someone who needs more grief support?
Help us reach more grieving hearts. Share
our site – www.garyroe.com.
We care for broken hearts.

THOUGHT QUESTIONS:

Who are the people who have been most helpful to you in your grief process? Are you spending enough time with them?

Are there certain people who are not helpful to you right now? Why? What have you done to limit your exposure to them?

Consider your Grief Recovery Team. Who are they? List them here:

What's the most important thing you think you learned from Part Two?

_____

_____

_____

_____

_____

_____

_____

_____

_____

PART THREE: LEANING FORWARD

There is something you must always remember.
You are braver than you believe, stronger than
you seem, and smarter than you think.

— A. A. Milne, *Winnie the Pooh*

58

THE REARVIEW MIRROR

Being stuck in grief is like driving a car
while looking in the rearview mirror.
You bump into things, and life hurts more.

A decade ago, my adoptive parents gave me a wonderful present: a rearview mirror.

I had just spent a week with them, processing some powerful events from my past. Months earlier, I began having flashbacks of sexual abuse from early childhood. The memories came out of nowhere, and the pain took over my life. Fortunately, I had a grief recovery team in place, and these folks may have saved my life. They certainly saved my sanity.

Healing was hard, exhausting work. I processed a theme park full of roller-coaster emotions. I sought counsel. I forgave, forgave, and forgave again. I began to release deep pain I had been carrying for decades. It wasn't pretty, but it was good.

As I shared my story and flashbacks with my adoptive parents, they were stunned, but not really surprised. Though they knew nothing of the abuse, they could look back and see the results in my life.

Before I got on the plane to return home, they presented me with the rearview mirror.

"Gary, let this be a reminder. You've done the hard work. Continue to glance in the rearview mirror as necessary, but it's time to gaze through the windshield. You have a wonderful future ahead," they said.

Glance in the rearview mirror as necessary and beneficial. Gaze through the windshield.

I am looking at that rearview mirror as I write. The past is so important, but we can't live there – not indefinitely. At some point, we have to turn in our seats and begin to look ahead.

LOOK AHEAD? HOW? WHEN?

There are times when we want things to change and we're eager to move on. But are we moving too fast? Are we getting ahead of ourselves? Are we taking our grief seriously?

Other times we don't want to move ahead. The world keeps spinning and we dig in our heels, screaming, "I'm not going!" Just the thought of looking forward feels wrong – like we're betraying or abandoning our departed partner.

Yet, no matter what situation we're in at the moment, or where we happen to be emotionally, deep down there is a wondering:

- What's next?
- What will my life be like?
- Who am I now? Who *will* I be?
- Will I make it?

When your mate died, he took part of you with him. Much of who you were was tied up in and influenced by him. With him gone, who are you now?

Your identity has taken a hit. It will take time to reconstruct who you are now, and who you will become.

So how do you know where to look – front or behind – and when?

Since your grief is an individual process completely unique to you, there are no hard and fast answers to these questions. But there are some guidelines.

First, you will not be perfect at this. No one is. In fact, I don't know what the perfect scenario would even look like. Your present and future are about making the best choices possible in your situation, based on what's happening in your own heart and the info you have available.

Second, if you focus on grieving well, you will heal and grow – no matter what. That can't help but be good. The more you heal, the better equipped you will be to reconstruct what you need to and lean into what's next.

Third, don't think about looking ahead and moving on as some one-time, big event. It's a daily, hourly, minute-by-minute, step-by-step process. As you listen to your heart and get the support and feedback you need, you'll look ahead naturally as time goes by.

LOOKING AHEAD IS ABOUT GRIEVING WELL

In terms of what you can do now, the answer is still the same: focus on grieving well.

Be aware of and acknowledge your emotions, whatever they are.

Build and utilize your grief recovery team.

Be with people who support you well and bring you comfort and peace.

Limit exposure to people who aren't helpful to you.

Make sure you have safe people with whom you can share deep feelings and fears.

Have access to grief, mental health, and medical professionals when you need them.

As you do this, things will become clear in their proper time.

Now, listen to the wisdom of your fellow widows and widowers. Learn from their experiences. This isn't an easy road, but it can still be good.

———◇———

Be nice to you.
Take your time. Don't be in a hurry.
And don't forget to breathe.

59
"IT FEELS LIKE YESTERDAY"

"It all seems so strange. I can still see him in his recliner. I still hear him in the kitchen. I dream about him at night," Ellen said.

"It's been eleven months, but it feels like yesterday."

Death messes with our sense of time. For a while, it's like life is in slow motion. Some people have memory gaps – periods of time during their grief that they don't remember at all.

It can seem like everything is happening at once, and life is flowing quickly past while you're standing still. Dazed, you see this activity but it doesn't seem to register somehow.

Everything is different, including your sense of time. Grief is like some weird alternate universe. The whole experience is surreal.

Time has a different meaning now.

"Weren't you here only a moment ago?
You seem so close sometimes."

Grief messes with our sense of time.

"Grief… Up till this I always had too little
time. Now there is nothing but time."

— C.S. Lewis, *A Grief Observed*

60
"SHOULDN'T I BE BETTER BY NOW?"

"How long is this going to take? Every morning I wake up to this cloud of up-and-down, unpredictable emotions. I drag myself out of bed wondering how I'm going to get through this day," Kathleen shared.

"Am I just feeling sorry for myself? Shouldn't I be better by now?" she asked.

Grief has no timetable.

You are unique. Your marriage and relationship with your partner was one-of-a-kind. Your grief process will be individual as well.

You won't grieve exactly like anyone else. It was *your* marriage.

You might wonder how long this is going to last. That's natural. It'll take as long as it needs to. You can't rush it, but you can focus on grieving in a healthy way.

Make grieving well a long-term commitment. You never know when grief will surface. Healing from deep wounds is often a lengthy process.

"My grief will last as long as it needs to. I'll never forget you."

King Solomon said,
"There is a time to mourn and a time to dance."
This is a time to mourn.
The time for dancing will come again one day.

61
"NO MAJOR DECISIONS!"

"*No major decisions!* I actually wrote that down and stuck it on the wall next to my bed," Brett stated.

"I've blown it twice already. I'm not myself and I'm not thinking straight. Nope. *I'm not making any more major decisions!*" he shouted, as if declaring his intentions to the world.

Brett learned the hard way. Soon after a loss usually isn't the time to make large, life-altering decisions.

You're in pain. You want to feel better. You want things to change. The temptation is to take control by changing something major. Some people…

- Seek a relationship
- Buy a new car
- Sell the house
- Move

Major changes are often an attempt to try and run from the pain of grief. This doesn't work. The grief is still there, waiting to be felt and processed.

> **"Now isn't the time for major decisions.**
> **I won't run from my grief."**

No major decisions?
For how long?
It depends.

Some grieve faster than others.

The general rule: wait a year before making major, life-changing decisions.

Your life has been altered enough for now.

The more you face your grief, the healthier you will be, and the better decisions you'll make.

62
"OUR ANNIVERSARY IS COMING UP"

"I don't know what to do. Our anniversary is coming up, and I'm dreading it. Every time I think about it, I break down in a puddle," Connie shared.

"It's like I'm paralyzed. I want to ignore it all together, but that seems disrespectful."

Anniversaries are hard. How could they not be? They were your special day together.

One thing is certain: your anniversary will come. Better to meet it head on and make some proactive decisions that can help unplug all that dread.

Decide beforehand who you want to be with that day, if anyone. Deliberately choose what you're going to do to honor your spouse and your late marriage.

Know that your anniversary will be hard, but it can also be good. How can you honor your loved one and use your anniversary to help you grieve?

Be nice to you. Your spouse would want that.

"Rather than dreading our anniversary, I'll use it to honor you and our marriage."

⟵◆⟶

Instead of dreading your anniversary,
use it to help you grieve.

How can you honor your spouse and your
relationship on that special day?

FOR REFLECTION AND/ OR JOURNALING

"When special days come, I hope that..."

_____

_____

_____

_____

_____

_____

_____

_____

_____

_____

_____

_____

63

"HER BIRTHDAY IS NEXT WEEK"

"Her birthday is next week. How am I going to survive that? I think I'll go crawl in a hole somewhere," Mick said.

Birthdays can be difficult. Memories flood in. Like Mick, you may want to hide.

Here's the truth: you can either use this special day, or it will use you.

How can you honor your mate on her day? What will you do to remember and give thanks for her? Did you have a birthday tradition of some kind? Can you somehow modify and keep it?

Celebrate your spouse on her birthday. Yes, it might be painful, but you'll be feeling the grief and processing it, rather than storing it up to sabotage you later.

Let her birthday remind you of the good times and produce thanksgiving. Think about and honor her.

Be proactive. You get to choose.

"I'll celebrate you on your birthday.

I'll use that day, rather than letting it use me."

⟨⟩

"What we have once enjoyed deeply we can never lose.

All that we love deeply becomes a part of us."

— Helen Keller

64
"HAPPY HOLIDAYS?"

"I went to the home improvement store this week and was greeted by what? Christmas decorations! I'm totally unprepared for that," Chris stated.

"Happy Holidays? Bah-humbug!" he said, rolling his eyes.

Holidays are the time when we look forward to gathering and celebrating together. It's also the time of year when we're most aware of who's missing. Holidays surface our losses. Reminders are everywhere. We bump into a memory with every step.

You can use the holidays to help you grieve. You can take charge and decide what you're going to do, how, and with whom. You can make specific plans for how you will include and honor your spouse.

Don't leave her as the elephant in the room. Remember her. Talk about and celebrate her. Share her with others.

It's okay to grieve at Christmas. Be real with your own heart. As you are, you'll be loving those around you and giving them a chance to grieve too.

"I'll use holidays to grieve well by
celebrating you and our life together."

Holiday grief is a huge issue.

It will hit not only this year, but every year.

For more on how to handle this time of year, check out...

Surviving the Holidays Without You: Navigating
Grief During Special Seasons.

65

"HOW CAN I GO ON WITHOUT HER?"

"People are telling me to move on. I can't do that. That seems cruel and heartless. How can I go on without her?" Greg asked.

"She's still with me. She's in here," he continued, tapping his chest. "I don't want to get over her. I can't."

People go on forever. You were one with your spouse. Your mate became a part of you. Losing them feels like losing a part of yourself.

Grieving isn't easy.

Perhaps some people are encouraging you to move on. Maybe you're feeling pressure to do that from within yourself. You know you have to lean forward sometime, but you're not sure what that looks like.

Let this be a comfort: it's impossible to move on *without* your loved one. You take your partner with you wherever you go. They're a part of you.

As you grieve, you'll discover how to move on *with* your spouse, but in new ways.

> *"I can't leave you behind. I'll move on*
> *with you, but in a new way."*

⋘⬥⋙

Grieving isn't about moving on without your spouse, but
discovering how to move on *with* them in new ways.

"Grieving is a journey that teaches us
how to love in a new way now that our
loved one is no longer with us."

— Tom Attig, *The Heart of Grief*

66

"HOW AM I GOING TO FIND THAT AGAIN?"

"Bill and I understood each other. We could just look at each other and *know*. How am I ever going to find that again?" Sarah sighed, rolling her eyes.

Your communication with your spouse was special and unique. Over time, you got used to that marital mental telepathy – where you understood each other without having to say a word.

You remember that look in your spouse's eyes. That smile. The immediate and intimate understanding. You did life together. *You just knew.*

That skill was years, perhaps decades in the making. Intimate understanding is wonderful to have and awful to lose.

The spouse you lost was one-of-a-kind. What you had was unique and special. You won't be able to duplicate it.

You may find such understanding again, but it will be different. Let the future be new. It can still be good.

> *"We were so good. I want that again,*
> *but I know it will be different."*

Don't try to duplicate what you had. You won't be able to.

Let the past honor your loved one. Let the
future be different. It can still be good.

"There is surely a future hope for you,
and your hope will not be cut off."

— Proverbs 23:18

FOR REFLECTION AND/ OR JOURNALING

"When I look ahead, I have hope that…"

_____

_____

_____

_____

_____

_____

_____

_____

_____

_____

_____

_____

_____

_____

67

"THE COLOR IS COMING BACK"

"I'm starting to enjoy some things. I'm even getting the urge for companionship. I'm starting to notice men again," Colleen shared, her mouth curled in a sheepish grin.

"There was a time when everything was dark. The color is starting to come back into life," she continued.

Many people feel some guilt at this stage. To re-engage in life and companionship can seem like a betrayal. Some spouses feel guilty for having even a tinge of happiness.

Picture your mate rejoicing. Your spouse would want you to be happy. It's okay to feel good. That's part of your reward for grieving well.

There will be a day when the fog begins to clear and you'll find yourself wanting to live again.

The color will return.

"I'm beginning to live again. I can almost see you smiling."

There will come a day when the fog begins to clear
and you find yourself wanting to live again.
The color will come back into life.

"I will turn their mourning into gladness; I will give them comfort and joy instead of sorrow."

— Jeremiah 31:13

68
"I'LL ALWAYS MISS HIM"

"I kept waiting for the pain to stop. Some things got easier with time, some didn't. Right now, there is this deep, dull ache in the recesses of my heart," Noel confided.

She paused and looked at her hands in her lap.

"I'll always miss him. Always," she said.

Yes, she will. You will too.

On some level, the ache in your heart will remain. You won't feel it as much, or as intensely perhaps, but it'll be there. When an aroma, place, or song triggers a memory, your heart will groan.

But over time, the ache will not only bring longing, but a smile. Thanksgiving for what you and your spouse had will replace some of the sadness over losing it.

Missing your spouse and leaning forward are not mutually exclusive. In fact, they go together.

Your mate has an always-place in your heart.

> *"I'll always miss you, because you have*
> *an always-place in my heart."*

"I still miss those I loved who are no longer with me
but I find I am grateful for having loved them.
The gratitude has finally conquered the loss."

— Rita Mae Brown

"But these three things remain: faith, hope, and love. But the greatest of these is love."

— 1 Corinthians 13:13

69
"I'M GOING TO MAKE IT"

"This has been harder than I would ever have dreamed. There's no way I could have known what it would be like. I've hurt like I've never hurt before," Brenda said.

"It's been a hard road, but I'm going to make it."

Losing a spouse is hard. Painful. Even devastating. You know.

Perhaps you've experienced pain as never before. Your heart was deeply wounded. You carry a unique ache with you in that place in your heart reserved for your mate.

You might not see much of the road ahead, but you know you're going to make it. After all, you survived this.

The pain will hit from time to time, but the memories will bring smiles too. Your spouse will begin to occupy his or her new place in your new normal. If you're willing, life can become more precious than ever.

> *"I don't know what's ahead, but I'm going to make it. I love you."*

———— ◆ ————

"He will wipe every tear from their eyes.
There will be no more death or mourning or crying or pain, for the old order of things has passed away."

— Revelation 21:4

Go ahead.
Lean forward.

FOR REFLECTION AND/ OR JOURNALING

"When I consider using my grief for good to serve others, I think of..."

_____

_____

_____

_____

_____

_____

_____

_____

_____

_____

_____

_____

70

"HOW LONG WILL THIS TAKE?"

"I didn't know grief could be such a long
and winding road. When does it end?"

— Cora, a widow

Grieving is hard and difficult work. It's draining and exhausting. Just when you think you're making progress, another trigger gets pulled and you feel like you're right back where you started. You naturally wonder, "When is this going to end?"

I've been asked perhaps hundreds of times by grieving hospice families, "How long will this take?"

The answer?

As long as it takes.

Grief has no timetable. And since your loss is one-of-a-kind (because you had a unique relationship with your spouse), your grief won't look exactly like anyone else's. Grief refuses to be boxed. It's ultimately about your heart and how you heal.

GRIEF SPIKES

"It's been five years. You would think I would be over this by now. I'm not. I still break down and cry. I still miss him when I walk through the kitchen. I still feel an ache deep in my heart when I see another couple holding hands," Marcia said.

Of course Marcia has these moments. She may have them all her life. But that doesn't mean she's doing something wrong or not healing. It means she misses her husband. That's natural. He has a special place in her heart reserved for him. When anything brushes that spot in her heart, she feels the ache of loss.

As far as I know, every widow and widower has what I call *grief spikes*. A hospice co-worker and bereavement coordinator calls them *grief bursts*. You're having a fairly routine day, and wham – you get hit with a sudden wave of grief.

Grief spikes are temporary. They manifest themselves in a variety of ways: crying, anger, deep sadness, chest tightness, fear, anxiety attacks, and even laughter. Most last a few moments and then are gone.

Grief spikes are normal. Sometimes you can identify the trigger – a song, aroma, place, etc. Other times, there seems to be no immediate cause at all. Grief spikes don't need a trigger. The grief resides in your heart, and is finding its way out, bit-by-bit.

Will you ever get it all out?

I don't think that's possible. Your heart has been wounded. The wound may heal well, but the scar will remain. Like a prior injury, the ache surfacing from time to time is natural and expected.

It's not about figuring out how to stop grieving or how to avoid grief bursts. The ache honors your spouse. Every grief spike says, "I loved you. I love you still." The scar is a gift – a reminder of the blessing you had.

Grief spikes aren't contrary to healing. In fact, they're a part of it. Your heart is expressing itself.

HEALING IS NOT AN EVENT

People look forward to the day when they will be healed. If we're talking about our hearts, I don't think that happens here in this life – at least not completely.

I've heard life described as a series of losses. I believe life is much more than this, but there is some truth in the statement. It's not a question of if we will lose someone, but when. How we respond to loss is vitally important. It becomes even more critical as our losses accumulate with time.

In other words, much of life becomes about our desire and willingness to heal.

Here are some things I have learned about healing:
- Healing is a journey, not a destination.
- Healing is a process, not an event.
- Healing takes place bit-by-bit, as you make proactive choices that are good for you.
- Healing happens as you pay attention to your heart and give it what it's needing.

None of us can say we're completely healed. But hopefully, we're healing.

Just as a death has ripple effects (your spouse's passing affected every part of your life), so do your choices to grieve well and to heal. You and those around you continue to benefit months and years later.

And as you heal, your heart will begin to expand. You have known deep pain and grief. Your experience can enable you to make a huge difference in the lives of others.

YOUR GRIEF HAS GREAT PURPOSE

Please know this: *your grief has great purpose.*

I don't believe grief and suffering should ever be wasted. Pain can be used for great good, if we're willing.

In other words, you can pay it forward. You can now use your grief experience to assist others. When you're ready.

You won't need to force this. You'll know when it's time.

Someone comes and asks how you got through this.

A friend experiences a similar loss.

You're sought out for your support and input.

You get an opportunity to volunteer.

Honor your loved one by giving back. Turn your grief toward greater purpose. You can multiply your love for your spouse by serving others.

SHARE THE HEALING

Many are hurting. And they can look into your eyes and know *you get it.*

Something happens when we're in the presence of a fellow sufferer who is safe. Our hearts begin to relax. Healing naturally begins to take place.

Focus on being a safe person. Accept people where they are as they are. Have no plans for their improvement. Don't try to fix them or help them feel better. Don't give advice they haven't asked for. Make your only agenda to walk alongside them in their valley.

In our hospice volunteer training, I talk about three keys to helping hurting people: show up, shut up, serve.

Show up. Show up in the lives of those who've been placed around you. Be aware. Hurting people need us to see them.

Shut up. Learn to be silent. Your presence is the most powerful gift you can give. We can embarrass ourselves quickly when we talk in the presence of great suffering.

Serve. Ask how you can help. What can you do for them?

You've been there. You know what this pain is like from the inside out. Again, you can't say you know how they feel, but you can relate and empathize.

As you participate in the healing grief of others, your heart will rejoice. Your pain has been used for good. Your grief takes on even deeper meaning and purpose. By helping others heal, you heal a little more yourself.

WE HEAL OVER TIME

How long is this going to take? This is a natural question, but it's one with no real answer. Perhaps because it's the wrong question.

A better question is this: *Are you healing over time?*

I'm not quite healed, but I am healing. I'll bet you are too.

Help us reach and help more broken hearts.
Share this link: https://www.garyroe.com/heartbroken-2/
Together, we can heal and grow.

THOUGHT QUESTIONS:

When you think of the future, what questions or fears do you have?

Which readings in Part Three meant the most to you and why?

How can you see yourself participating in the healing of others?

What is the most important thing you think you learned from Part Three?

_____

_____

_____

_____

_____

_____

_____

_____

_____

_____

_____

SOME FINAL THOUGHTS

You've just been on a difficult journey. You've experienced some powerful emotions, and perhaps some disturbing thoughts. You've had new insights, and perhaps some of your questions have been answered.

Hopefully these words from fellow widows and widowers have engaged your heart and comforted your soul. Perhaps you can now say the following with more confidence:

"I'm not alone."

"I'm not crazy."

"I'm going to make it."

In some ways, you'll never stop grieving. You'll always miss your mate. You love them.

TAKE CARE OF YOU

The grief road can be long. Along the way:

- Be nice to yourself. You've been hit hard.
- Be patient. Take your time.
- Feel your emotions as they come.
- Get the alone time you need, but stay connected to others.
- Build and use your Grief Recovery Team. You need them.

Lean forward.

Grieve well.

And don't forget to breathe.

SUMMARY OF AFFIRMATIONS

"I don't want this to be real. I love you too much."

"I'm stunned. I should be. I'll breathe deeply and be kind to myself."

"Grief is a marathon. I'll remember you, and pace myself well."

"My heart is torn because it is one with yours. This is painful."

"I'll learn to pay attention to what I'm feeling. This is part of honoring you."

"You were just here. How could you be gone?"

"My grief is deeper than I imagined, but I can meet it with courage today."

"Nothing could prepare me for losing you. I feel your absence everywhere."

"The pain is astounding. How could it not be? I love you."

"I'm numb. Where did you go? I love you."

"I may get anxious, but that doesn't mean I'm in danger. It will pass."

"Grief is exhausting. I'll honor you by taking care of me."

"You were the air I breathed. Your absence is like a lack of oxygen."

"You're my best friend. Life will be so different without you."

"I need to grieve both what I lost and what I never had."

"Everything seems to remind me of you. I'll learn to treasure each memory."

"Without you, I feel lost, but answers will come as I need them."

"I miss your voice, but I hear it deep inside. I'll treasure your words."

"I'm not crazy, but life without you is."

"I'll honor you by forgiving myself for what I did and didn't do."

"I miss you, but I'm relieved you're not suffering anymore."

"I'll take the questions of my heart seriously, including 'Why?'"

"It hurts that I can no longer come home to you. I feel your absence everywhere."

"I'll cherish the little things I miss about you. I never want to forget them."

"I'm sorry I took you for granted. Please forgive me. I'm so thankful for you."

"When I feel angry, I'll honor you by expressing it well."

"I lost you slowly and in pieces. No wonder my grief feels so fragmented."

"When things feel unfair, I'll focus on honoring you and on grieving well."

"I may experience some depression. This is natural. I miss you."

"Losing you feels wrong. I'll find positive ways to express my anger."

"Even little things seem huge without you. Grief can be overwhelming."

"My life has changed forever. You're that special to me."

"My dreams are shattered. I'll grieve in healthy ways and retool the future when it's time."

"I can't imagine life without you, but somehow I'll find a way to live with even greater meaning and purpose."

"It's okay if I feel devastated. You were my home."

"Everything feels so heavy. You mean even more to me than I knew."

"I will seek helpful, safe people and avoid unhelpful, judgmental voices."

"Even our pet is in mourning. We miss you."

"I can be with my kids in their grief and still grieve well. We can do this together."

"My kids are hurting too. I'll help them find the support they need."

"Family is so important. Rather than comparing and competing, I'll find ways to cooperate."

"I'll forgive quickly and surround myself with helpful influences."

"We were unique and special. I'm so thankful for you."

"I'll find and trust some safe people. They'll help me recover and heal."

"I'll take the alone time I need, while being careful not to isolate myself."

"My heart is torn from losing you. This naturally affects all my relationships."

"I'll listen, but not let others push me. I'll take my time making decisions."

"I'll never get over you, but I will get through this season of grief."

"I'm more vulnerable than I know. I'll take my time and heal."

"I don't expect everyone to understand, but I do need a few trusted allies for this fight."

"I'll let others love me. This helps all of us."

"I'll find some people who know grief. We can navigate this together."

"Others are feeling similar pain. We can help each other."

"Weren't you here only a moment ago? You seem so close sometimes."

"My grief will last as long as it needs to. I'll never forget you."

"Now isn't the time for major decisions. I won't run from my grief."

"Rather than dreading our anniversary, I'll use it to honor you and our marriage."

"I'll celebrate you on your birthday. I'll use that day, rather than letting it use me."

"I'll use holidays to grieve well by celebrating you and our life together."

"I can't leave you behind. I'll move on with you, but in a new way."

"We were so good. I want that again. but I know it will be different."

"I'm beginning to live again. I can almost see you smiling."

"I'll always miss you because you have an always-place in my heart."

"I don't know what's ahead, but I'm going to make it. I love you."

ALSO FOR BEREAVED SPOUSES

COMFORT FOR THE GRIEVING SPOUSE'S HEART: HOPE AND HEALING AFTER LOSING YOUR PARTNER

"Compassionate. Comforting. Healing. Readers will see them-selves on every page."

> \- Paul Casale, Licensed Professional Counselor,
> Marriage & Family Therapist

"Bereaved spouses will find help, hope, and healing in these pages."

> \- Dr. Charles W. Page MD,
> Author of *A Spoonful of Courage*

THIS LOSS CHANGES EVERYTHING.

The loss of a life partner can be traumatic. Oblivious to our suffering, the world around us speeds on as if nothing happened. Stunned, shocked, sad, confused, and angry, we blink in disbelief. Our hearts are broken. Our souls shake.

Written with heartfelt compassion, this warm, easy-to-read, and practical book reads like a caring conversation with a friend and will become a comforting companion as you navigate the turbulent waters of grief.

Gary's desire is to meet you in your grief and walk with you there. Composed of brief chapters, *Comfort for the Grieving Spouse's Heart* is designed to be read one chapter per day, giving you bite-sized bits of comfort, encouragement, and healing over time.

In *Comfort for the Grieving Spouse's Heart*, you will discover how to...

- Process complicated grief emotions (sadness, anger, guilt, confusion, guilt, anxiety, depression, feeling overwhelmed, etc).
- Navigate all the relational changes - feeling alone, misunderstood, isolated, and even rejected by those around you.
- Handle the increased stress and uncertainty that this heavy loss can bring.
- Deal with physical and mental health issues, illnesses, and new symptoms that often arise.
- Take care of yourself through diet, hydration, fitness, and rest.
- Deal with a myriad of practical issues (financial challenges, parenting, family activities),
- Handle the intense, deep loneliness that often comes with this loss.

You will also find hope in how to...

- Think through the challenging spiritual and faith questions that frequently surface.
- Relate well to the people around you - those who are helpful and those who aren't.
- Overcome the tendency to run from emotional pain with unhealthy habits or compulsive behaviors.
- Deal well with triggers and the grief bursts that will come.
- Find the support you need for survival, recovery, and healing (safe people, fellow grievers, counseling, etc.).

- Develop a simple, realistic plan for birthdays, anniversaries, and holidays.
- Use your grief for good - for yourself, your family, and others.
- Allow this loss to give you greater perspective and motivate you to live more effectively than ever before.
- Make your life count, one day, one moment at a time.

Don't grieve alone. Let *Comfort for the Grieving Spouse's Heart* join you on this arduous, tasking journey.

www.garyroe.com/comfort-series

ADDITIONAL RESOURCES

BOOKS

AFTERMATH: PICKING UP THE PIECES AFTER A SUICIDE

Painful. Traumatic. Confusing. Complicated. No chance to say goodbye. No final embrace, kiss, or touch. No opportunity to clear the air, ask and give forgiveness, or make amends. The suicide tsunami has come, and now you're left standing amid the aftermath. This book is designed to be a companion for those grieving a suicide death, offering comfort, perspective, hope, and healing. Gary walks with you through all the emotional, mental, physical, spiritual, and relational upheaval that comes with a suicide loss. Let Gary journey with you through the aftermath and help you pick up the pieces and begin to rebuild your heart and life. *Aftermath* is available in various formats from most book retailers. www.garyroe.com/aftermath

DIFFERENCE MAKER: OVERCOMING ADVERSITY AND TURNING PAIN INTO PURPOSE, EVERY DAY

You've been hit and wounded. Life hasn't turned out to be what you expected, wanted, or hoped for. Your heart says, "There has to be more." Yes, there is. It's time to turn things around, expose the lies you've been fed about yourself, and embrace the truth. You're a Difference Maker - and it's time to start living that way. In *Difference Maker*, you'll discover how to conquer obstacles like fear, anxiety, anger, depression, and self-destructive behavior. You'll learn why you're here, what your mission is, and how to live with more purpose and passion than you dreamed possible. *Difference Maker* is available in adult and teen editions in various formats from most online book distributors. www.garyroe.com/difference-maker

COMFORT FOR GRIEVING HEARTS: HOPE AND ENCOURAGEMENT FOR TIMES OF LOSS

We look for comfort. We long for it. Grieving hearts need it to survive. Written with heartfelt compassion, this easy-to-read, warm, and practical book reads like a caring conversation with a friend and is destined to become a classic for those looking for hope and encouragement in times of loss. Composed of brief chapters, **Comfort for Grieving Hearts** is designed to be read one chapter per day, giving you bite-sized bits of comfort, encouragement, and healing over time. Available through most major online book retailers. For more information or to download a free excerpt, visit www.garyroe.com.

TEEN GRIEF: CARING FOR THE GRIEVING TEENAGE HEART

Teens are hurting. While trying to make sense of an increasingly confusing and troubled world, teens get hit, again and again. Edgy, fun-loving, tech-driven, and seemingly indestructible, their souls are shaking. We can't afford to allow pain and loss to get the better of them. Written at the request of parents, teachers, coaches, and school counselors, this informative, practical book is replete with guidance, insight, and ideas for assisting teens navigate the turbulent waters of loss. *Teen Grief* is a Winner of the 2018 Book Excellence Award and has received rave reviews from those who live and work with teens. *Teen Grief* is available in both paperback and electronic versions. For more information or to download a free excerpt, visit www.garyroe.com.

SHATTERED: SURVIVING THE LOSS OF A CHILD

Unthinkable. Unbelievable. Heartbreaking. Whatever words we choose, they all fall far short of the reality. The loss of a child is a terrible thing. How do we survive this? Written at the request of grieving parents and grandparents, *Shattered* has been called "one of the most comprehensive and practical grief books available." The book combines personal stories, compassionate guidance, and practical suggestions/exercises designed to help shattered hearts navigate this devastating loss. *Shattered* has received sterling reviews by both mental health professionals and grieving parents. It is available in various versions at most major online book retailers. For more information or a free excerpt, visit www.garyroe.com.

PLEASE BE PATIENT, I'M GRIEVING: HOW TO CARE FOR AND SUPPORT THE GRIEVING HEART

People often feel misunderstood, judged, and even rejected during a time of loss. This makes matters more difficult for an already broken heart. It doesn't have to be this way. It's time we took the grieving heart seriously. Gary wrote this book by request to help others better understand and support grieving hearts, and to help grieving hearts understand themselves. A group discussion guide is included. *Please Be Patient, I'm Grieving* is a Best Book Awards Finalist. It can be found in various formats at most major online bookstores. For more info or a free excerpt, visit www.garyroe.com.

SURVIVING THE HOLIDAYS WITHOUT YOU: NAVIGATING LOSS DURING SPECIAL SEASONS

This warm and intensely practical volume has been dubbed a "Survival Kit for Holidays." It has helped many understand why holidays are especially hard while grieving and how to navigate them with greater confidence. Being proactive and having a plan can make all the difference. An Amazon holiday bestseller, *Surviving the Holidays Without You* was a Book Excellence Award Finalist. Available in various formats at most major online retailers. For more info or to download a free excerpt, visit www.garyroe.com.

SAYING GOODBYE: FACING THE LOSS OF A LOVED ONE

Full of stories, this warm, easy-to-read, and beautifully illustrated gift book has comforted thousands. It reads like a conversation with a close friend, giving wise counsel and hope to those facing a loss. Co-authored with *New York Times' Bestseller* Cecil Murphey, this attractive hardback edition is available at www.garyroe.com/saying-goodbye

FREE ON GARY'S WEBSITE

THE GOOD GRIEF MINI-COURSE

Full of personal stories, inspirational content, and practical assignments, this 8-session mini-course is designed to help readers understand grief and deal with its roller-coaster emotions. Several thousand have been through this course, which is now being used in support groups as well. Available at https://www.garyroe.com/good-grief-mini-course/.

THE HOLE IN MY HEART: TACKLING GRIEF'S TOUGH QUESTIONS

This powerful e-book tackles some of grief's big questions: "How did this happen?" "Why?" "Am I crazy?" "Am I normal?" "Will this get any easier?" plus others. Written in the first person, it engages and comforts the heart. Available at https://www.garyroe.com/the-hole-in-my-heart/

I MISS YOU: A HOLIDAY SURVIVAL KIT

Thousands have downloaded this brief, easy-to-read, and very personal e-book. *I Miss You* provides some basic, simple tools on how to use holiday and special times to grieve well and love those around you. Available at https://www.garyroe.com/i-miss-you/

OTHER RESOURCES:

GriefShare:
www.griefshare.org

The Grief Toolbox:
www.thegrieftoolbox.com

Open to Hope:
www.opentohope.com

A REQUEST FROM
THE AUTHOR

Thank you for taking your heart seriously and reading *Heartbroken: Healing from the Loss of a Spouse*. I hope you found some comfort, healing, and practical help in its pages. I would love to hear what you thought of the book. Would you consider taking a moment and sending me a few sentences on how *Heartbroken* impacted you? Send me your thoughts at contact@garyroe.com. Your comments and feedback mean a lot to me and will assist me in producing more quality resources for grieving hearts. Thank you.

Warmly,
Gary

Visit Gary at www.garyroe.com and connect with him on Facebook, Twitter, LinkedIn, and Pinterest

Facebook: https://www.facebook.com/garyroeauthor
Twitter: https://twitter.com/GaryRoeAuthor
LinkedIn: https://www.linkedin.com/in/garyroeauthor
Pinterest: https://www.pinterest.com/garyroe79/

ABOUT THE AUTHOR

Gary's story began with a childhood of mixed messages and sexual abuse. This was followed by other losses and numerous grief experiences.

Ultimately, a painful past led Gary into a life of helping wounded people heal and grow. A former college minister, missionary in Japan, entrepreneur in Hawaii, and pastor in Texas and Washington, he now serves as a writer, speaker, chaplain, and grief counselor.

In addition to *Heartbroken*, Gary is the author of numerous books, including the award-winning bestsellers *Shattered: Surviving the Loss of a Child*, *Comfort for the Grieving Spouse's Heart*, and *Aftermath: Picking Up the Pieces After a Suicide*. Gary's books have won three national book awards and have been named as finalists eight times. He has been featured on Dr. Laura, Belief Net, the Christian Broadcasting Network, Wellness, Thrive Global, and other major media and has well over 700 grief-related articles in print. Recipient of the Diane Duncam Award for Excellence in Hospice Care, Gary is a popular keynote, conference, and seminar speaker at a wide variety of venues.

Gary loves being a husband and father. He has seven adopted children, including three daughters from Colombia. He enjoys hockey, corny jokes, good puns, and colorful Hawaiian shirts. Gary and his wife Jen and family live in Texas.

Visit Gary at www.garyroe.com.

Don't forget to download your free, printable PDF: *Healing Wisdom from Heartbroken* https://www.garyroe.com/wisdom-from-heartbroken

AN URGENT PLEA

HELP OTHER GRIEVING HEARTS

Dear Reader,

Others are hurting and grieving today. You can help. How?

With a simple, heartfelt review.

Could you take a few moments and write a 1-3 sentence review of *Heartbroken* and leave it on the retailer's site?

Just go find *Heartbroken* on the retailer's site and then click on "Customer Reviews" just under the title.

And if you want to help even more, you could leave the same review on the *Heartbroken* book page on Goodreads.

Your review counts and will help reach others who could benefit from this book. Thanks for considering this. I read these reviews as well, and your comments and feedback assist me in producing more quality resources for grieving hearts.

Thank you!
Warmly,
Gary